When Black Men Stretch Their Hands to God

Messages Affirming the Biblical Black Heritage

George O. McCalep, Jr., Ph.D.

Foreword by
Wm. Dwight McKissic, Sr.

Orman Press
Lithonia, Georgia

When Black Men Stretch Their Hands to God
Messages Affirming the Biblical Black Heritage

by
George O. McCalep, Jr., Ph.D.

Copyright © 2003
Orman Press, Inc.

ISBN: 1-891773-50-X

Scripture quotations are taken from THE HOLY BIBLE, *King James Version,* or are the author's paraphrase of that version.

Printed in the United States of America

10 9 8 7 6 5 4 3 2 1

Orman Press, Inc.
Lithonia, Georgia

DEDICATION

I dedicate this book to the black church and the black preacher. I believe that the most effective institution for disseminating truth is the black church and the most qualified vessel to deliver the truth is the black preacher. Therefore, I dedicate this book to them with the hope and prayer that they will receive the foundational prophecy, and preach and teach these spiritual truths in pulpits and Christian education ministries across the country. I also dedicate this book to the biblical scholars, especially the new breed of outstanding theologians, whose research has made a practical book like this possible.

TABLE OF CONTENTS

Foreword I

Preface 1

PART I: THE PROPHECY

When Black Men Stretch Their Hands to God 23
Cushites Rejoicing in the Land of Ham 31

PART II: CHRIST-CENTERED LESSONS FROM BIBLICAL BLACK CHARACTERS

The First and Last Adam 47
From Ham to Canaan 55
From Canaan to Abraham 69
From Nimrod to Pentecost 77
From Phut to the Cross 89
From the Ethiopian Eunuch to Passover 101
From the Cradle to the Cross 111
Christ-Centered Lessons from Biblical Black Women 131

PART III: THE PRAYER OF A BLACK MAN NAMED JABEZ (A KENITE)

Lord, Bless Me Indeed! 147
Enlarge My Coast, Increase My Territory, and That Thine
    Hand Might Be With Me 155
Keep Me from Evil That It May Not Grieve Me 161
The Bookends of Jabez's Prayer .169

PART IV: A GOODLY HERITAGE

Claiming Our Goodly Heritage 181
A Change in the Order 189
God Understands Ebonics 199
The Voice of the Blood of the Slaughtered 209

PART V: SAMARITANS IN THE BIBLE

A Good Black Samaritan 219

PART VI: THE CUSHITE MOVEMENT

The Cushite Movement 233

APPENDIX

"What Shall I Tell My Children Who Are Black?"
by Margaret Taylor Goss Burroughs .244

"Man, Oh Man, How Wonderful You Are!"
by Angela J. Williams 246

Notes 247

Bibliography 249

FOREWORD

Dr. George McCalep is convinced from Scripture that God desires to send a spiritual awakening and revival to black men in America and throughout the African Diaspora (people of African descent spread throughout the world in these last days). *Spiritual awakening* has been defined as "an outpouring of the Spirit of God upon His people that divinely enables them to live lives that are godly, to love each other unconditionally, to serve the Lord productively, to praise Him appropriately, to rejoice in Him plentifully, and to witness for Him convincingly." *Revival* has been defined as "a fresh touch or movement of God among His people that awakens the church and impacts the world." I share Dr. McCalep's view that Psalms 68:31 is a prophetic verse that can only be fulfilled through descendants of Ethiopians or Cushites, which I believe encompasses modern day African-American men. God promised to send a spiritual awakening to this world before His son returns (Acts 2:17).

The Bible provides a prophetic portrait of an eschatological (end times) spiritual awakening among God's people that specifically includes people of African descent (Psalm 68:31, Acts 2:17, Zeph. 3:10, Hos. 6:3, Is. 66:19–20).

We will see a major change in America "when black men stretch their hands to God." The day will come when black men in America, on a large scale, will stretch out their hands to God. This is the revival or spiritual awakening that we prayerfully await—when multiple thousands or even several million African-American men and Caucasian men "lift up holy hands without wrath and dissension" (1 Tim. 2:8). We see this happening in pockets and places, but the day will come when black men in America on a large scale will stretch out their hands to God. When this revival hits black America, it will have an impact upon America similar to the first and second Great Awakenings and the Azusa Street Revival of 1906. The Great Awakenings were a watershed even in the life of the American people. Before it was over, they had swept the colonies of the eastern seaboard, transforming the social and religious life of land. My prayer is that the Lord will do it again and use this book to help awaken black men in America. For black men and white men to lay aside their *dissensions* and *wrath* and worship Jesus together on a large scale, that truly will be evidence of revival in our land. Let me say it again: We will see a spiritual awakening in America, perhaps like never before seen in history when BLACK MEN STRETCH THEIR HANDS TO GOD. As a matter of fact, whenever we see multiple thousands of men gather together to worship Jesus and the audience is thoroughly balanced racially, we will know that a spiritual awakening and revival have come to America.

Dr. McCalep has labored diligently in this writing to be biblically based, theologically true, anthropologically accurate, historically honest, exegetically enlightening, cross-culturally relevant and spiritually impactful. This book not only affirms a black presence in Scripture, but challenges all men, and particularly black men, to live Christ-centered lives. Every black adult male who reads this book will be enhanced in his Christian and cultural identity and challenged to live up to the standards set by our biblical forefathers. Every non-African American who reads this book will better understand our hurts and hopes; our pains and gains and ultimately relate to us better. If this book is read and applied by all men, our wives will have better husbands, our children will have better fathers, our mothers and fathers will have better sons, our churches will have stronger men and race relations will be improved.

David Dewitt says there are three stages of manhood—boy, man and patriarch. All males obviously experience the boy stage. The man and patriarchal stages are only experienced by those who meet certain criteria. The patriarchal stage involves having enough resources to not only meet the needs of your immediate family, but to also minister to and meet the needs of others in your circle of contact and influence.

Dr. McCalep truly is a patriarch among us. This book is just one of the many resources from one of the most resourceful men I know to elevate, evangelize and edify God's people and to participate in the Davidic prophecy that the Ethiopians will stretch out their hands to God. I pray that descendants of Ethiopian men who are patriarchs among us would utilize their resources to make sure African-American men and boys have a copy of this book and live up to its challenges.

I would love to see this book inspire a Cushite/Caucasian Christ-centered movement that will reach multitudes (perhaps millions) in spiritual awakening rallies across this country. These rallies would fulfill Paul's desire that men in every place would pray (1 Tim. 2:8); David's pronouncement that Ethiopians would stretch our their hands to God (Psalm 68:31); Jesus' challenge that "If I be lifted up, I'll draw all men unto Me" (John 12:32) and His prayer that "they might be one" (John 17:21). My prayer is that God would use this book to bring revival to our land. David prayed, "Will you not revive us again, that your people may rejoice in you" (Psalm 85:6).

Dr. George McCalep's writings reflect the critical thinking skills of an academic scholar, the heart of a pastor, the fire and fervor of an evangelist and the tenacity and forthrightness of a prophet. Dr. McCalep's book accurately and eloquently affirms a black presence in Scripture. However, more importantly, this book inspires and encourages black men to worship and obey God in Spirit and truth for the Father seeketh such to worship Him (John 4:23, 24).

May I close with prayer: Lord, would you let each person who reads this book experience revival in his heart, home and church, that spills into the community and eventually sweeps our nation, all for your glory and honor, in Jesus' name. Amen.

Rev. Wm. Dwight McKissic, Sr.
Senior Pastor
Cornerstone Baptist Church
Arlington, Texas

PREFACE

The Prophecy

God has given me a prophecy. I have never considered myself a prophet in the sense of being able to foretell the future. However, a prophet is one who receives and declares a word from the Lord. Because God is sovereign, He can give a word of prophecy to whomever He wishes, and whenever He desires to do so. God has given me a word of prophecy and said tell it. The prophecy is:

> When black men stretch their hands to God in submission and adoration, God will bring an unparalleled revival to all His people.

In Psalm 68:31, which I interpret to be a processional, it reads, *"Princes shall come out of Egypt; Ethiopia shall soon stretch out her hands to God."* This is not a black church revival, but rather a revival of ALL of God's children—black white, brown, red and yellow. God wants to use the most oppressed, discriminated people in the world to bring about a revival for ALL of His people. God has always used the most unlikely to accomplish great things for His glory, such as little David slaying big Goliath, or allowing Peter to preach at Pentecost, or me to write this book and pastor His church.

Now God wants to use children of former slaves that represent the most discriminated human specimen on earth to lead an unsurpassed revival.

It is my prayer that this book will result in not only black men, but all people receiving this prophecy and eventually experiencing its fulfillment.

What This Book Is Not About

The purpose of this book is not to promote racism or separatism. This statement will be repeated throughout this book because, unfortunately, any discussion regarding people of color in the Bible tends to fuel the fire of racism. This is a Christian book written by a born-again man who tries daily to pick up the cross, follow Christ and walk not in the flesh, but in the spirit, in pursuit of love for all people.

> *The purpose of this book is not to promote racism or separatism.*

I am not white bashing. I will never do so; nor will I permit it in my presence. As a matter of fact, I believe that African Americans need to invite other races of people to church, especially whites. Some of us bypass many opportunities to win souls for Jesus just because the person is of another race. God never said that black people should go and compel only black people. He just said to go. The problem is that too many of us are prejudice. I am talking about black prejudice.

What This Book Is About

The purpose of this book is to affirm the black biblical heritage that has been ignored, misconstrued, misinterpreted and, in some cases, entirely removed. Its aim is to eradicate ignorance, correct racist interpretations, and affirm the existence of the rich heritage and presence of black people in the Bible. The ultimate purpose of this book is to provide a prepared channel of vessels for God to usher in a revival for all people.

> *The purpose of this book is to affirm the black biblical heritage that has been ignored, misconstrued, misinterpreted and, in some cases, entirely removed.*

The classic definition of revival is "to resuscitate; to impart life; to renew; to regain; and to restore vitality and effectiveness." I expect a spiritual awakening in the local church and throughout God's land as a result of people reading this book, preachers preaching its message and teachers teaching its content. This truth needs uncovering. My intention is to simply restore, revive and liberate us with the truthful Word of God. The Bible tells us that we shall know the truth and the truth shall set us free (John 8:32).

This book is designed to teach us some biblical black history. God is no respecter of persons. There is no black or white in God. There is no Jew or Gentile in God. We are members of a holy race and the human race. God has told us that if any man is in Christ, he is a new creature and that the old has passed away, and all things are made new (2 Cor. 5:17). This simply means that if we are Christians, no matter how we have been treated in the past, we have no right to harbor hatred in our hearts against anyone. No matter how I was treated in my home state of Alabama, and no matter how many times I was called the "n" word by little white children, as a Christian, I cannot and should not allow any racial bias or hatred to reside in my heart.

When my wife and I were in Australia, we listened to our tour guide tell the history of Australia and how the Europeans had come and taken over the native Aborigines. The tour guide told of how the Aborigines were mistreated much like America mistreated our Native Indians. A good friend of mine who happened to be a European Caucasian brother was also listening. I could see his head begin to drop as the guide talked about how his people had treated the Aborigines. Once the tour guide was done, I looked at my friend and he looked at me. I put my arms around him and hugged him. He returned to me a gentle hug. I then said to him, "Brother, if any man is in Christ, he is a new creature. The old is gone. Because of Jesus there is only the new." He said, "Thank you, Jesus!" And I said, "Thank you Jesus!" We need to thank Jesus for making us new creatures.

According to courthouse books in Alabama and other southern states, and the United States Census Bureau (until 1979), if a person has one iota of black blood, he or she is officially considered black.

Black Defined

Anytime we use a descriptive word like the word *black*, we need to have a descriptive definition. I need to give my definition of black; otherwise, the debate and argument of the word *black* could go on and on. My definition of *black* differs from the one I was given as a young man in Alabama. According to courthouse books in Alabama and other southern states, and the United States Census Bureau (until 1979), if a person has one iota of black blood, he or she is officially considered black. That means that if anyone in the family genealogy of either the mother or father is black, then all of the offspring are black. It is called "The One Drop Theory."

> *I would like to define black, from a working theological framework, as a descriptive word for both ancient and modern people. It refers to an "African bloodline, with any combination or degree of discernible African features."*

My definition of *black* includes the One Drop Theory, but is slightly broader. I would like to define *black*, from a working theological framework, as a descriptive word for both ancient and modern people. It refers to an "African bloodline, with any combination or degree of discernible African features," which means a whole lot of biblical people are going to be black according to my definition.

Moses, David, Solomon, the Queen of Sheba, Mary of Nazareth, Paul, and even Jesus, are black according to my definition. No, Jesus did not escape the African bloodline.

Mary, the mother of Jesus, as well as Joseph, Jesus' earthly father, came from David, who had an African bloodline. Therefore, Jesus was black, according to my definition of black.

According to my observation while visiting various cathedrals in the Holy Land, the pictures of Jesus, Mary and other biblical characters were black in the early century until a new trend was started. Pope Julius II commissioned Michelangelo to paint Jesus white. Later, Leonardo da Vinci did the same. It is hard for us to accept a black Madonna and Christ. Could it be that in our minds nothing as good as Jesus and God could be black?

People will probably criticize my definition of black because it does not mention race, but race as we know it today is a relatively new concept. There were not any races in the Bible, but nations of people. Around 1500 B.C., some racism existed based on rivalry, competition and territory, not white supremacy.

I know that God is spirit and that we are made in His spiritual likeness. Yet, for whatever reason, God decided to reveal His divine self in color. Ezekiel tells of Jesus sitting on the throne. He described Jesus' appearance from the waist up as bronze. Daniel had another vision of Jesus and described God's hair as wool. In John's revelation of Jesus, he said that he did not see Jesus' body, but he saw His feet and they were brown. If the Father and the Son are one, then they must be of one color also, and that is brown.

Jesus is the Word who became flesh. Whenever something becomes flesh it has to be of some kind of color. We cannot escape this fact and say that Jesus is spirit. Jesus had to look like something because He became flesh. We believe He was fully man, so He could not walk around looking like nothing. It is time we let the truth set us free. God truly called His son out of Africa (Egypt) (Hosea 11:1, Matt. 2:15).

Seven Important Facts

Fact 1: People who do not know their past do not have a future.

Fact 2: It is unrealistic and unreasonable to expect another culture to lift up our culture. It is irrational to think that the Oriental or European culture will honor the African culture. If we do not value our own culture, then no one will. Other races are too busy lifting up their own culture. Why should we expect them to lift up ours?

Fact 3: Culturally speaking, integration is an unrealistic joke, a myth and nearly impossible. The definition of the word *integrate* defies cultural integration. To integrate means to make something new from parts of something old. To integrate culture is like trying to mix tacos, ribs, spaghetti and potatoes together. But once we are done mixing, we do not have a new entity; we still have tacos,

> *Jesus is the Word who became flesh. Whenever something becomes flesh it has to be of some kind of color.*

ribs, spaghetti and potatoes. We may have blacks and whites going to school together, which is fine, we fought for that; but the word integration was wrong from the beginning because it defies culture. We cannot integrate cultures.

Fact 4: We cannot be free of slavery because of our ignorance. The problem I have with Black History Month is that it does not go far enough into the past. It is built on the ideology that black history began with slavery. When I was in school, we learned about Mary McCloud Bethune, Thurgood Marshall, Wilma Rudolph, Jackie Robinson, Charles Drew and Benjamin Bannaker. We learned little about the Egyptians, such as Queen Nefertiti and Ramses. We did not learn of Saint Augustine of Hippo and Quintus Tertullian of Carthage, the fathers of Christianity. More tragically, we learned absolutely nothing about biblical black history and heritage. Most of us believe that Africans became Christians after slavery. However, Tertullian became a Christian before AD 197.

> *The curse of Ham is a lie. The world has used the curse of Ham to explain our blackness.*

Tertullian of Carthage (c. 160 - 225) is considered one of the fathers of Christianity. Tertullian was black. He was the son of a centurion and trained as a lawyer in Rome. Tertullian was denounced for his view that philosophy is of the world's wisdom and that the Lord should be sought through simplicity of heart.

Additionally, many of us have not been set free from our own prejudice. If we do not like white people, then we have not been set free. The truth brings about reconciliation, effective multiculturalism and liberation. The truth will set everyone free. When the Son of God set us free, He made us free indeed.

Fact 5: The curse of Ham is a lie. The world has used the curse of Ham to explain our blackness. It is a racist lie. It is one of the biggest lies ever told and the Ku Klux Klan was founded upon it. I am going to dispel the lie here and now.

The lie says in the beginning, starting with Adam, everyone was white. The lie goes on to say that Noah cursed Ham and he became black. White America did the research before we did. They understood the truth before we discovered it and chose to hide it. They told us that Noah cursed him and made him black. First, Noah did not curse Ham; he cursed Canaan, Ham's son. Noah

> *Noah could not have made Ham black because he was already black.*

was angry because his youngest son, Ham, saw him naked and drunk in his tent and told his older brothers. Noah was so angry that he cursed Ham's son, Canaan, to be a servant to Shem and Japheth (Gen. 9:18–27). Evidence of the Canaanites' servitude is seen later in Joshua 9:23 and Judges 1:28.

The name *Ham* means "black." Ham was the original ancestor of the Cushites (Ethiopians), Egyptians and Canaanites. According to biblical time lines, Ham had been black for one hundred years before he looked upon his father's nakedness. So Noah could not have made Ham black because he was already black.

Biblically speaking God never cursed anyone and turned them black, however on two occasions, He did curse someone and turned them white. When Elijah's servant was cursed, God turned him white with leprosy (2 Kings 5:20–27). Likewise, Moses' sister, Miriam, was cursed with leprosy and turned white as snow (Num. 12:10). The two times God changed someone's color in the Bible, He turned them white.

The curse of Ham is referenced in the following resources:

- *The Layman's Bible* (1964)
- *Broadman Bible Commentary* (1969)
- *Wesleyan Bible Commentary* (1975)
- *Wycliffe Bible Encyclopedia* (1975), page 746
- *Nelson Illustrated Bible Dictionary*, page 454
- *Encyclopedia Britannica* (1992), Volume 8, page 737

There is a great debate in our school systems about whether or not we should teach biblical creation or Darwin's theory of evolution. I believe there should be another fight to get any reference to the curse of Ham out of books. As long as this curse is referenced in books that hold great credibility like the *Encyclopedia Britannica* that most children use when doing their homework, our children will continue to be brainwashed. (An extensive discussion on the Curse of Ham can be found in the chapter entitled "From Ham to Canaan.")

> *As long as this curse is referenced in books that hold great credibility like the **Encyclopedia Britannica** that most children use when doing their homework, our children will continue to be brainwashed.*

Fact 6: The current ills of our black community, such as violence, crime, drugs, lack of motivation, high school dropouts and low academic achievement scores are only symptoms of a people who have been taught self-hate. All the trauma and drama we are experiencing in the black community today are symptoms, not the root of the problem. The root of the problem is a stolen identity that has separated us from our God, our Creator, and resulted in a cultural identity crisis and self-hatred.

Fact 7: Our young people's minds are being attacked through misguided education. If we did not have modern technology such as cameras and videos, several hundred years from now, somebody would say that Martin Luther King, Jr. was white, just as they claim the Egyptians were white.

> *A misguided education of what it means to be black eventually leads to self-hate.*

We have been tremendously brainwashed and it continues on our young people. They are undergoing what I call *psychic assault*. Politics, the media, and even theology, are attacking their very minds. A misguided education of what it means to be black eventually leads to self-hate.

Racism Today

Today, racism has changed its form. It is packaged differently than it was when I was growing up. It looks so differently today that if we don't watch closely, we will think it does not exist. In my day, there were physical lynchings, but today the weapon of racism is mental lynching. Again, our children's very psyche is being attacked.

I never had my mind attacked. I grew up knowing who I was and whose I was. When I grew up, I was concerned about my body, but not my mind. I knew I should not walk through a place called Lincoln Mills at a certain time of night. I also knew that I could not whistle at a white girl. I was concerned about my physical well-being, but today, the concern is the mind. My mind and spirituality have never been attacked like my sons' have. Suicide was almost unheard of for my age group, but today it is common to young black people whose minds are being assaulted.

In prayer meeting, we sometimes talk about the things our children are going through. A parent once shared an incident regarding his son who was in an accelerated class, in DeKalb County, Georgia, in 1994. His son went to class one day, but the teacher sent him to the principal's office. When it was all straightened out, the teacher explained that she didn't expect him to be in an accelerated geometry class. My elder son can remember his experience at Clarkston High School. He came home from school one day and said "Dad if they give me that test one more time, I'm going to know it by heart." He was making such a high score on the test that the teachers thought he was cheating. My youngest son while attending Woodward Academy, supposedly an integrated multicultural school, began to grow a mustache when he turned thirteen years old. The academy personnel told him that he had to cut it off, so he could look like them although it made him vulnerable to keloids, a skin disease to which many black men are predisposed. So I raised a question: "Why can't he look like his daddy instead of looking like these other daddies?" The sad note was that even the African-American people agreed that he had a choice either to cut it or be put out of school. This did not sound like a multicultural school to me. His mind was literally being attacked for who he was, and even his own people could not understand it.

Black Is Beautiful!

Black is beautiful; however, western civilization and American-European culture infer that black is bad or ugly. For example, undesirable people are put on a *black list*. A bad child in the family is called the *black sheep*. Any crime of extortion is labeled *black mail*. We say that judging someone wrongly is *the pot calling the kettle black*. In the movies, the good guys always wear white hats and the bad guys wear *black hats*. On October 19, 1987, the stock market took a nose dive, and that day is forever known as *Black Monday*. A white lie is considered okay and not really a lie, but a real whopper of a lie is a *black lie*. When we go to the bakery and ask for angel food cake, we get white cake, but when we ask for devil food cake, we get *black cake*. We have been and are still being brainwashed.

> *Black is beautiful, however western civilization and American-European culture infer that black is bad or ugly.*

Why have we been told that bodily hair is ugly? When I was in college at Alabama A&M University, a big hairy-legged girl was fine. Now, black girls shave their legs. We have been brainwashed into thinking that bodily hair is not only ugly, but also nasty. We are undergoing an assault upon our minds.

Our young people are under attack. They don't know whose they are, and we don't have any sympathy for them. Why? Because we have never had our minds attacked like theirs are being attacked today. They don't know who they are spiritually or psychologically. Only the truth will set them free. If the Son of God sets them free, they will be free indeed.

What Color Is God?

God is spirit and not flesh. Who told us God was white? Did we read it in the Bible? The world's perception is that God is white. It is because the untruth that His Son was a blue eyed, blond-haired white person has been promoted for centuries. Therefore, the inference is that God must be white because Jesus and the Father are one. If we used that same reasoning to acknowledge the truth that the historical Jesus was a man of color, we would conclude that God is black. God is spirit, but no one ever claims Him as spirit until someone else claims Him as black. Why do I have to defend God as black, but no one ever has to defend Him as white?

> *God is spirit, but no one ever claims Him as spirit until someone else claims Him as black. Why do I have to defend God as black, but no one ever has to defend Him as white?*

What does this mean? It means that we are trying to set the record straight relative to our black biblical heritage. It means we are trying to eradicate the brainwashing and mis-education that has assaulted the minds of black Americans and led them to bondage, self-hate and destruction. It means that God loved us so much that He revealed Himself like us, which means we ought to love ourselves, not hate ourselves. It means that when we hurt each other with black-on-black crime, we are hurting those who are like God. It means that when a black brother kills another black brother or sister, or calls a sister the "B" word, it's the same as talking about Jesus. He was a brother, too. It means that we are made in God's likeness, and if there are any attributes that are good, then they are in us. God is good and so are we. We are made in His image.

In addition, it means that we are trying to liberate the entire Christian faith from a lie and cover up that hold us in bondage. How can we, as Christians, be all that God wants us to be when we, like Enron and other corporate giants, are guilty of perverting the truth? To deny blacks the heritage and lineage from Adam, Noah and Ham is sinful. To deny the African bloodline of the historical Savior of the world is a sin and a shame.

What Is In This Book?

The messages set forth in this book are intended to address all of the issues, problems and concerns set forth in this introductory chapter. The book is divided into the following sections:

Part I: The Prophecy

The first section focuses on what God has inspired me to tell the world, and what is set forth in the title of this book, and that is: When black men stretch their hands in submission and adoration, God will bring an unparalleled revival to all His people. These messages give the foundation upon which the prophecy is based. They describe what will happen in the lives of God's people when black men stretch forth their hands to God in praise and adoration.

Part II: Christ-Centered Lessons from Biblical Black Characters

This section focuses directly on the primary intent of this book, which is affirming our biblical black heritage.

Part III: The Prayer of a Black Man Named Jabez (A Kenite)

In 1 Chronicles 2:55, we find a place named Jabez that was inhabited by the Kenites. If we associate the man, Jabez, with the place, Jabez, we can reasonably assume that the man was a Kenite. The Kenites are descendants of the black Hamitic blood line. Genesis 15:19 lists the Kenites with the Canaanites and other inhabitants of the land of Canaan. First Chronicles 2:55 tells

> *When Black men stretch their hands in submission and adoration, God will bring a revival to all of His people.*

us that the Kenites were scribes. This is significant to the role of black people in God's unfolding plan of redemption. According to Ernest Sargent III, "Over a hundred years ago, German scholars brought a document from the land of Judah known as the *Kenite Manuscript* to the world's attention. Sargent further states:

> "The targum of 1 Chronicles 4:12 states, 'These were the men of the Great Sanhedrin.' Without a doubt, one of Jethro's greatest contributions to Moses and Israel was his legal advice suggesting the instituting of the counsel of seventy elders, which became the Great Sanhedrin (Numbers 11:16). From this vantage point, it appears that Jabez may be the priestly president, presiding over the Great Sanhedrin. Perhaps a better translation of "the scribes, which dwelt at Jabez," might be the scribes which convened around Jabez (1 Chronicles 2:55)."[1]

Many people have prayed the prayer of Jabez in recent years and, more importantly, thousands have given testimonies of life changing experiences because of it. I am compelled to wonder if Jabez' prayer would have received the same degree of popularity and acceptance if the world had known it was a black man's prayer.

> *I am compelled to wonder if Jabez' prayer would have received the same degree of popularity and acceptance if the world had known it was a black man's prayer.*

Bruce Wilkinson found a golden nugget in a little prayer hidden in the Old Testament of God's Word, in the book of 1 Chronicles. He wrote a book about it which he entitled The *Prayer of Jabez*.

The intent of these messages in this book is to propose that what God did for Jabez, the Kenite, He will do for you.

Part IV: A Goodly Heritage

This is a collection of messages that further affirm who we are and whose we are. They speak to the rich inheritance we have first as Christians and then as African Americans. Unlike the previous sections this is not a sermon series. These are individual messages that were preached during Black History Month. The only continuity that they have is their focus on the same general theme. These messages are designed to inform, motivate and encourage.

Part V: Samaritans in the Bible

This is a study from my book, *A Good Black Samaritan*. This writing was designed to teach us how Jesus used people of color to teach the entire world what is good. An examination of Scripture relative to the origin of the Samaritans indicates they are from the lineage of Ham, and therefore descendants of a black man. This study specifically looks at three Samaritans who are mentioned in the New Testament. As we study these Samaritans, we will find several traits that should be exemplified in all believers.

> *Jesus used people of color to teach the entire world what is good.*

Aside from the three Samaritans, I took a deeper look at the town of the Samaritans who believed in the Word of God in the book of Acts. As we investigate the lives of these people of color, I pray that some will be comforted, others enlightened and many set free and delivered.

Part VI: The Cushite Movement

The final section of the book introduces the Cushite Movement, a men's ministry whose ultimate goal is to bring a God-given prophecy to fruition.

This book is not a theology book on the black presence in the Bible. Rather, it is written and designed for the average reader to enjoy while being enlightened on this very serious subject of our biblical black heritage.

I want to encourage preachers to preach these very critical messages. The Bible says, "How can they hear without a preacher?" (Rom. 10:14). The Sunday pulpit hour has always proven to be one of the best avenues of communication. The information contained in these messages is crucial to the survival of the black race and essential to the Christian faith.

In addition, the book is an excellent resource for Bible studies and small group book studies. Each section includes a study guide for this purpose. Read, study, teach, preach and observe the transforming power of God's truth as myths and ignorance are eliminated, chains are broken and burdens are lifted as God's people are set free.

Part I:

The Prophecy

WHEN BLACK MEN STRETCH THEIR HANDS TO GOD

Psalm 68:1–4 (NIV)

¹May God arise, may his enemies be scattered; may his foes flee before him. ²As smoke is blown away by the wind, may you blow them away; as wax melts before the fire, may the wicked perish before God. ³But may the righteous be glad and rejoice before God; may they be happy and joyful. ⁴Sing to God, sing praise to his name, extol him who rides on the clouds—his name is the Lord—and rejoice before him.

Psalm 68:11(NIV)

The Lord announced the word, and great was the company of those who proclaimed it.

Psalm 68:31–32(NIV)

³¹Envoys will come from Egypt; Cush will submit herself to God. ³²Sing to God, O kingdoms of the earth, sing praise to the Lord, Selah.

Psalm 68:35

You are awesome, O God, in your sanctuary; the God of Israel gives power and strength to his people. Praise be to God!

Threading the black woman has always been out front by necessity. During slavery, when the master came to the slave's front door, the male slave could not go out to greet him. If he did, he would have been killed because he would have been perceived as being haughty. Instead, the black woman had to go out and greet the "masa." The black woman has always been our leader and we thank God for the sisters who went forth when we could not.

The enemy knows that in order to destroy a culture, you need to get rid of its males. That is why Pharaoh sought to kill all of the first-born Israelite males.

> The enemy knows that in order to destroy a culture, you need to get rid of its males.

If the enemy knows that the way to destroy a culture is by getting rid of its males, then the Church needs to know that the only way to put society and the church back together is through its men. When black men stretch their hands to God in praise, there will be a revival in the church and the nation.

When Revival Comes

God has poured a prophecy into my spirit that I am to proclaim to all the world. The prophecy is: When black men stretch their hands to God in submission and adoration, God will bring an unparalleled revival to all His people. When Black men stretch their hands to God in praise, God will arise in the Church and in the hearts of the lost. When black men begin to stretch their hands to God in praise, there will be a movement in the land.

Psalm 68:31 (KJV) says, *"Princes shall come out of Egypt; Ethiopia shall soon stretch out her hands unto God."* The words *Ethiopia* (Gen. 2:13) and *Cush* (Gen. 10:6) are used interchangeably in the Bible. The word *Cush* means "black" in Hebrew.[2] *Ethiopia* is the Greek word for Cush and means burnt-face; not pale-face, but burnt-face, like us. Burnt-face men shall stretch out their hands, open up their mouths and sing to God in praise. Try to imagine it with me. It is not only about black men in choirs stretching out their hands to God in praise, but all men. Men stretching out their hands to God in praise has to begin with our church leadership. Imagine all the deacons in the church marching in a procession into the sanctuary, lifting up their hands to God and singing songs of praise. Can you see it? Imagine all male ushers opening the worship service with their hands stretched to God in praise, singing "Let God Arise and His enemies be Scattered." Can you see it?

Nearly fifty percent of the people in the congregation where I pastor are males. Imagine all these men stretching out their hands to God in praise and submitting themselves to Him—the Cushites praising God and singing His songs. One day there is going to be a movement. Can you see it?

This is not a men's only message, it is a word for the church. Women should encourage the men in their lives to stretch out their hands to God in praise, for when they do, they will make better husbands, fathers and lovers. Most of us men are not good at expressing our love for the people we love, but we have no problem expressing our love for things, such as sports and business. God is calling men to stretch out their hands to Him in praise so that they will be all that God wants them to be.

A question to the women is: "When you see black men stretching their hands to God, what will be your response?" I believe most women of God will respond, "Yes, Lord! Thank you, Lord!"

What Happens When God Arises?

When God arises the enemy is scattered and there will be a healing in the land. If we want the enemy to scatter, then we should let God arise. The psalmist uses the word *smoke* in Psalm 68:2 to describe God's arising. We have seen smoke go up and be driven away by the wind. It is the same when God arises and the enemy is driven away. We want to get rid of the drug addicts, dope pushers, pimps and carjackers in our neighbor-

> *When God arises the enemy is scattered and there will be a healing in the land.*

hoods, but we are going about it the wrong way. I appreciate the police, but the Bible tells us that if we let God arise, our enemies will be scattered. Just as a candle will burn itself up, so shall it be with the enemies of God when He arises.

When God arises the righteous will be glad. I do not understand how Christians who are saved do not rejoice over it. About fifty percent of most congregations sit in their seats and do not rejoice at all when people come to Christ. I have a hard time understanding that. Some even look at their watches or walk out when preachers offer the invitation to Christ. What could be more important than saving a person from the depths of the fiery lake of hell? I have come to believe that the watch-watchers might be saved because they tend to rejoice when their wives, husbands or children get saved. Perhaps, they are not interested in anyone other than their loved ones getting saved. I don't know, but the Bible tells us that when God arises in the hearts of the saints, we ought to rejoice.

When God arises, Christians ought to be glad. Has God ever risen in your life? If God has risen in your life, then you ought to be glad about it. A songwriter wrote:

> "Come those who love the Lord
> Let their joys be known.
> Join in a song of sweet accord
> And thus surround the throne.
> Let those refuse to sing
> Who never knew our Lord,
> But children of the heavenly King
> Will sing their joys abroad."

If God has been good to us, then we ought to say so. If God has delivered us or healed our bodies, we ought to say so. If we have ever experienced God's love, power, grace or mercy, we ought to say so. When God arises, the people of God should rejoice and be glad because the third thing that happens when God arises is strength and power are given to His people. Nehemiah said it best when he wrote, *"The joy of the Lord is your strength" (Neh. 8:10).*

When Does God Arise?

According to Psalm 68:11, God arises when many teach His word. Pastors and preachers should not be responsible for all the teaching and preaching in the church. Many should make the Word known, not only should pastors, preachers and teachers witness and share the gospel, but every believer.

God spoke a word to me about witnessing. God has commanded that the church grow. He has told us to go into the entire world to teach and baptize in His name, and He would be with us even unto the end of the earth (Matt. 28:19–20). The last thing Jesus told us to do before He returned to heaven was *"Go."*

Some of us want only the preachers or deacons to go, but God didn't say, "Preachers and deacons go." He just said, "Go." God arises when many publish the Word. Everyone should be a disciple, a follower of God and a follower of Christ, walking in His steps. God says there is no such thing as being a church member who just comes to church on Sunday. God wants all believers to be disciples and witnesses for Him everywhere we go.

> *God also arises when His name is blessed.*

God also arises when His name is blessed. In Psalm 68:26, the psalmist tells us to bless God in the congregation. He concluded in Psalm 68:35 by saying, *"Blessed be God."* In the earlier verses, the psalmist talks about why we should bless God. For instance, in verse 5, he assures us that God is a father to the fatherless and a defender of the widows. Verse 6 assures us that God places the lonely in a family. Verse 9 tells us that God brings forth rain in dry and weary times. That is why in Psalm 103, the psalmist writes: *"Bless the Lord, O my soul: and all that is within me, bless his holy name. Bless the Lord, O my soul, and forget not all his benefits"* (Psalm 103:2–3). When we think of the goodness of Jesus and all that He has done for us, our very souls should cry out, "Hallelujah!"

Summary

God arises when His people stretch their hands to Him in praise, His Word is taught by many and His name is blessed. That means that God will arise when the burnt-faced men who are descendants of the Cushites of Africa stretch out their hands, open their mouths and sing praises to Him.

The psalmist says in Psalm 68:31 that princes will come out of Egypt. God-fearing, burnt-faced men from Africa will come stretching out their hands to God in praise. The Cushites will surrender themselves to God. The purpose of stretching our hands to God is to show our submission to Him. The NIV version of the Bible says, *"Cush will submit herself to God"* (Psalm 68:31).

Men of color and all men need to stretch their hands to God and all men. We need to give God *yadah* praise, which means "to show adoration." We need to give God *towdah* praise, which means "to let God's blessings come down." All around the world, up-lifted hands is a universal sign of surrender. If someone walks up to us, points something in our backs and says, "Stick 'em up!" our hands automatically go up. God is saying, "Stick 'em up! I want the body of Christ—

men, women and children—to give me yadah and towdah praise. I want the body of Christ to publish my Word and be witnesses to all the world. I want the body of Christ to bless my name. Then, I will rise and bring a revival to my people. I will give them strength and power. I will heal their land."

CUSHITES REJOICING IN THE LAND OF HAM

Psalm 68:25–27(NIV)

[25]In front are the singers, after them the musicians; with them are the maidens playing tambourines. [26]Praise God in the great congregation; praise the Lord in the assembly of Israel. [27]There is the little tribe of Benjamin, leading them, there the great throng of Judah's princes, and there the princes of Zebulun and of Naphtali.

Psalm 106:21–23 (KJV)

[21]They forgot God their saviour, which had done great things in Egypt; [22]Wondrous works in the land of Ham, and terrible things by the Red sea. [23]Therefore he said that he would destroy them, had not Moses his chosen stood before him in the breach, to turn away his wrath, lest he should destroy them.

In Psalm 68:24–35, the psalmist David describes a processional of all the tribes and nations of the universe marching into the temple before the Lord. The procession begins at verse 25, which tells us that the singers were in front followed by the musicians who were followed by girls playing timbrels or tambourines. Next, all the congregation began praising God saying, "Praise God in this great congregation."

Verse 27 tells us that the tribes with their rulers were next in the procession. First, there was Benjamin from Bethlehem and one of the two sons of Rachel and Jacob. Second was Judah, the tribe of praise, the tribe of Jesus. The Lion of Judah came praising, marching and singing, "Praise God in this great congregation." Zebulon, ugly Leah's sixth child, was there singing too. Lastly, there was Naphtali, Jacob's child who was born out of wedlock. Some of us can identify with him because some of us were born out of wedlock. Then, Psalm 68:31 tells us the Ethiopians, the sons of Ham, the burnt-faced men, shall soon stretch out their hands to God in praise, acknowledging Him for His wondrous works.

God's Wondrous Works

I propose that God wants all of us, and particularly, those of us who are of African descent, to praise Him for His wondrous works. Why? Because He has blessed us with an experience that deserves praise. If anybody in this country should praise God, it should be black people. After all, we are, in many cases, one generation removed from educational opportunities, poverty and the Jim Crow laws of segregation. We are only one generation from back door entrances to restaurants,

STAR
POINT

separate waiting rooms in doctors' offices and separate bathroom and water fountains labeled "colored only."

When my wife and I went on our honeymoon, we drove many miles to find a hotel room that would accept us. We were rejected and denied by many hotels because of the color of our skin, not our character. But God brought us through all of that and by His wondrous work, we found a place that would accept us.

God wants black people to stretch forth our hands to acknowledge and praise Him for the wondrous works He has done for us. God particularly wants black men to praise Him because black men are the most discriminated, rejected and denied species on the face of the earth. Yet God has raised us up and we have overcome the obstacles that beset us. Therefore, we ought to be witnesses for Him. God wants the Cushites to witness to the whole world. He wants the Cushites to come forth so the world can see

> *God particularly wants black men to praise Him because black men are the most discriminated, rejected and denied species on the face of the earth.*

our hands stretched out to Him in praise, giving Him glory and acknowledging Him for His wondrous work of bringing us over the obstacles.

Identifying People of Color in the Bible

The Bible and God are completely color blind. God does not say that this person is a person of color, so he or she should or should not be blessed. God is not interested in that. Over the years, European culture has projected nearly all biblical characters as European or white, although the geographic setting of the Old and New Testament is Africa and Asia. It is really asinine to think that only Europeans are in Africa and Asia.

Because God is color blind in His Word, we have to depend upon the geographic location and name to help us identify people of color in the Bible. Genesis 10 tells us that after the flood, Noah had three sons: Ham, Japheth, and Shem. The name *Ham* means "dark or black." The name *Shem* means "dusky or olive-colored." The name *Japheth* means "bright or fair."[3]

> *Because God is color blind in His Word, we have to depend upon the geographic location and name to help us identify people of color in the Bible.*

Japheth's descendants inhabited Asia Minor. The Japhetic people included the Medes, Greeks, Cypriots and probably the Caucasian people of Europe and northern Asia. Some scholars include Orientals in this group.

Shem's descendants are the Semitic people who occupied Syria or the area near the upper part of the Euphrates River. The Semitic people include the Jews, Arabs, Assyrians, Arameans and Phoenicians. Abraham was a Shemite or Semite.

Ham's descendants settled in the eastern part of North Africa and the coastal regions of Canaan and Syria. Ham was the original ancestor of the Cushites (Ethiopians), Egyptians, Canaanites, Philistines, Babylonians, Jebusites, Amorites,

Girgasites and Hivites. Biblical scholars unanimously agree that the children of Ham are the darker people of color who dwelled in the land of Ham and are referred to in the text.

Genesis 10:6 tells us that the sons of Ham were Cush, Mizraim, Phut and Canaan. Mizraim means Egypt, which was also a tribe of the nation that dwelt in the continent of Africa and ruled it at that time. Egypt, despite what Hollywood has depicted is in Africa and was occupied by Africans. The Middle East is divided between Africa and Asia. The Middle East is not a continent. The Middle East is on the continents of Africa and Asia.

> *The travel of God's people, the children of Israel, was in the land of Ham or Egypt. Egypt is in Africa, and at that time, only Africans lived in Africa*

The travel of God's people, the children of Israel, was in the land of Ham or Egypt. Egypt is in Africa, and at that time, only Africans lived in Africa—Africans who looked like many of us, and were mixed colors like us. Yes, many of them look like us, with dark skin full of melanin, good obedient kinky hair and marvelous broad noses.

Why Praise God?

David tells us in Psalm 106 that the people of God have forgotten how God helped and blessed them in Egypt, at the Red Sea and in the land of Ham. The text focuses on a variety of reasons as to why Israel should praise God.

First, David told the Israelites that they should praise God for the great things He did for them in Egypt. It seems a strange praise for the Israelites to give. Was David saying to praise God for four hundred years of slavery and making bricks in the mud to build great pyramids in the sun under the master's whip? How were these things great? God blessed them in the land of Goshen, northeast of the Nile Delta. It was a land that was supposed to be uninhabitable. No one was supposed to be able to live there; yet, the Israelites were assigned to live there. They found refuge in the land of Goshen and at least one million of them miraculously survived. God was telling the Israelites to praise Him for blessing them in Egypt because he made them into a strong nation and blessed them with a deliverer, Moses, while they were under the master's whip.

STAR
POINT

David also told the Israelites that they should rejoice for the terrible things God did at the Red Sea. The word *terrible* has two meanings. *Terrible* in this passage of Scripture means "great." The destruction of Pharaoh's army at the Red Sea was a great act by God. The significance of the text is that the Israelites' backs were up against the wall. Pharaoh's army was coming down upon them and the Red Sea was ahead of them. When we look at the geography, we see that God could have led them another way, but He intentionally led them to the Red Sea. Then He worked a terrible, wonderful act. He opened the Red Sea and they crossed to the other side. Then, He closed the Red Sea on the enemy. David said the Israelites should praise God for His wondrous acts at the Red Sea.

Finally, David told the Israelites that they should praise God for His wondrous works in the land of Ham. All during the Israelites' travel in Egypt and Canaan, God blessed them. He did wondrous things. He provided quail six days out of every week. He provided water from a dry, hard rock. He pushed back the Jordan River and allowed them to cross over into the best part of the land of Ham. He knocked down the walls of Jericho in the land of Ham. The Israelites should praise God for the great things that He did in Egypt, by the Red Sea and in the land of Ham.

The Black and Israelite Experiences

The black (Cushite) experience and the Israelite experience parallel each other. God has done wondrous works for us, like He did for the Israelites in the land of Ham. Most of us have survived in uninhabitable places like Goshen. We have survived in places where nobody else could make it. We survived the slave ships that brought our forefathers and mothers from our native land. We survived the master's plantation. We survived having our women raped and our men whipped and lynched. We survived the cotton, peanut and tobacco fields. We survived living on the other side of the railroad track in every city in America. We survived in the land of Goshen and some of us are still

> *The black (Cushite) experience and the Israelite experience parallel each other. Like the Israelites, we ought to praise God for our Red Sea experiences.*

surviving there. David is saying that twenty-first century Cushites ought to praise God for blessing us to survive in a land that was uninhabitable.

Like the Israelites, we ought to praise God for our Red Sea experiences. We have seen the Red Sea of segregation rolled back. We have seen the Red Sea of Jim Crow rolled back. We have seen the Red Sea of second-class citizenship rolled back.

> *Like the Israelites, the Cushites have a problem. We have forgotten that it was God who kept us in our awful land of Goshen.*

We have seen the Lord make a way out of no way when our backs were up against the wall. We didn't know how we were going to get out, but God stepped in and rescued us. We, the twenty-first century Cushites, ought to praise God for our Red Sea experiences.

Like the Israelites, we ought to praise God for the wondrous works He has done in the land of Ham. God is still tearing down Jericho-walls. He is tearing down walls of addiction in the land of Ham that is full of crack cocaine and other substance abuse. God is still tearing down strongholds and bringing deliverance.

Don't Forget God

Like the Israelites, the Cushites have a problem. We have forgotten that it was God who kept us in our awful land of Goshen. God blessed us, helped us and made a way out of no way for us in our Red Sea experiences. Just like the Israelites, we have forgotten the wondrous works that God did in our land of Ham. We can see this in ourselves when we come to church Sunday after Sunday and fail to stretch our hands to God and acknowledge and praise Him for His wondrous works.

We should never forget what the Lord has done. When we count our blessings, we may discover or even be surprised about what the Lord has done. Look at what He has done today.

Blessing One: The blood is still running warm in our veins.

Blessing Two: We are still on this side of the Jordan River.

Blessing Three: We are not pushing up daisies.

Blessing Four: We have bread on our tables.

Blessing Five: We have a roof over our heads.

This is only a minor listing of our corporate blessings, but the truth is that the list is infinite. Count your blessings. Name them one by one, and then discover what the Lord has done. Didn't He bless us in the ghetto and project houses? Didn't He bless us on the farms? Didn't He bless us in the tobacco and cotton fields? Didn't He bless us in the land of Goshen, by the Red Sea and by the land of Ham?

Ungodly Black Male Pride

The Holy Spirit allowed me to see another problem hidden in the text. I have labeled it "ungodly black male pride." The text tells us that princes, sons of kings and soon to be kings and rulers of Egypt, came forth. God showed me that for a true revival to come forth in this country, big-time black men in high positions, such as doctors, lawyers, business owners, CPAs, CEOs, supervisors in corporate America and more, will have to let go of their egos and come forth with their hands stretched out to God in praise. Too often black men in high positions forget who put them there. They begin to think that they are self-made men.

The black man's mentality has to step down out of the high lofty places in order for a true revival to take place. The black man's mentality has to come out of corporate America and those high military rankings with their hands stretched to God in praise. When black men who have risen already, come forth with their hands stretched to God, praising and acknowledging Him for whom He is, God will bring a true, unparalleled revival to all His people.

> *God has taught us, the children of Ham and Cush, to expect deliverance at the Red Sea.*

God needs black men to be His witnesses. He needs the Cushites to come forth rejoicing and praising with their hands stretched out to Him. Why? Because it is a witness to Scripture when we stretch our hands to God. Everyone needs to know that we love the Lord. When we stand up and stretch our hands to Him, the world will know.

Protecting Our Future

God has taught us, the children of Ham and Cush, to expect deliverance at the Red Sea. It is a blessing to know that when our backs are up against the wall, God will show up and show out. When it looks like there is no way out, God will show up. God has prepared me to just look for Him. I have come to know that He is always there and coming to my rescue. If I just wait on Him, He will come. God has taught me through my Red Sea experiences that if He does it once, He will do it again. I am convinced that when all odds are against us and there is no way out, we can look up and there will be God.

But consider those who have not been taught to expect deliverance when they come to their Red Sea experiences. The Cushites of my age have been blessed to experience that God will make a way out of no way, but we have not taught this to our children. Psalm 106:23 says:

> *"Therefore he said that he would destroy them, had not Moses his chosen stood before him in the breach, to turn away his wrath, lest he should destroy them."*

The new Cushite generation needs to know that God will make a way out of no way, but the only way they can know it is for us to teach them. We cannot let our children be destroyed. We must talk to them about God and the wondrous works He has done. They need to see our hands stretching to Him in praise.

When a daddy who makes six figures and lives in a big house comes forth with his hands stretched out to God, his children might ask him, "Daddy, how can you be so excited about this God that you have never seen?" Then he can tell them God can make a way out of no way. Some young lady who has gotten pregnant and is thinking about taking her life and that of her

> *The Cushites of my age have been blessed to experience that God will make a way out of no way, but we have not taught this to our children.*

unborn child needs to know that God will make a way out of no way. A young man who has flunked out of college and is ashamed to go home needs to know that it does not matter what our situation is, there is a God. Our young people need to know that there is a God who can make a way out of no way, and He will show up and show out.

Summary

If we can think, we can thank. If we can thank, we can praise. If we can praise, we can worship. God is a color blind God. He does not care if we are black, red, brown or white. God wants everybody to praise Him. If He has been good to us, then we ought to praise Him. Let everyone come forth with outstretched hands praising the Lord. If the Lord has blessed us in the land of Goshen, by the Red Sea and in the land of Ham, then we ought to stretch our hands to Him in praise. Let us count our blessings. He died for all. He was raised for all. He can save all and He can deliver all. Let the Cushites rejoice in the land of Ham. Let everybody and everything that hath breath praise the Lord!

Part I: The Prophecy
Study and Review

1. Why does God want black men to stretch their hands to Him?

   God wants the men from whom He began civilization and through whom He brought His Son into the world to be a model of submission and adoration for all mankind. God wants to use the most oppressed people of the world to bring restoration to all of His people.

2. What will happen if black men stretch their hands to God?

   When black men stretch their hands to God, He will bring an unparalleled revival to ALL of His people. In stretching our hands to God, we will bring about reconciliation and healing for families, all races and God's church. When black men stretch their hands to God in praise and adoration, there will be a movement in the land.

3. How have we been brainwashed regarding our biblical black heritage?

   European whites and the media have whitewashed biblical characters to remove all resemblance to Negroid features. They have denied our African ancestry and the rightful place of people of color in the Bible. Stealing our heritage has left black people not knowing their value to God or their place in history. This loss has resulted in centuries of self-hate and destruction.

4. Why is it important to teach our children that our God will show up in Red Sea experiences?

Our children need to know that the God we serve will be with them in all of life's situations, no matter how difficult or bleak they may be. Our children need to know that the God we serve will make a way out of no way. If our children do not trust God for their survival, then Satan will surely destroy them.

5. The prophecy is "When black men stretch their hands to God, God will bring an unparalleled revival to all His people." How will God's people be revived and why will it be for *all* His people?

God's people will be revived through reconciliation, first with Him and secondly with each other. When black men accept the place for which God created them, they will finally be able to lift their heads and truly love themselves. They will freely lift their hands in praise and adoration for a Creator who so wonderfully and magnificently made them. Black men represent the most oppressed beings in our world. When those who are most oppressed can show love and forgiveness toward their oppressor, they will model God's love and reconciliation for all of His people.

Key Point

Part II:

Christ-Centered Lessons
from Biblical Black Characters

THE FIRST AND LAST ADAM

Genesis 1:27

So God created man in his own image, in the image of God created he him; male and female created he them.

Genesis 2:7–25

[7]And the Lord God formed man of the dust of the ground, and breathed into his nostrils the breath of life; and man became a living soul. [8]And the Lord God planted a garden eastward in Eden; and there he put the man whom he had formed. [9]And out of the ground made the Lord God to grow every tree that is pleasant to the sight, and good for food; the tree of life also in the midst of the garden, and the tree of knowledge of good and evil. [10]And a river went out of Eden to water the garden; and from thence it was parted, and became into four heads. [11]The name of the first is Pison: that is it which compasseth the whole land of Havilah, where there is gold; [12]And the gold of that land is good: there is bdellium and the onyx stone. [13]And the name of the second river is Gihon: the same is it that compasseth the whole land of Ethiopia. [14]And the name of the third river is Hiddekel: that is it which goeth toward the east of Assyria. And the fourth river is Euphrates. [15]And the Lord God took the man, and put him into the garden of Eden to dress it and to keep it. [16]And the Lord God commanded the man, saying, Of every tree of the garden thou mayest freely eat: [17]But of the tree of the knowledge of good and evil, thou shalt not eat of it: for in the day that thou eatest thereof thou shalt surely die. [18]And the Lord God said, It is not good that the man should be alone; I will make him an help meet for him. [19]And out of the ground the Lord God formed every beast of the field, and every fowl of the air; and brought them unto Adam to see what he would call them: and whatsoever Adam called every living creature, that was the name thereof. [20]And Adam gave

names to all cattle, and to the fowl of the air, and to every beast of the field; but for Adam there was not found a help meet for him. [21]And the Lord God caused a deep sleep to fall upon Adam, and he slept: and he took one of his ribs, and closed up the flesh instead thereof; [22]And the rib, which the Lord God had taken from man, made he a woman, and brought her unto the man. [23]And Adam said, This is now bone of my bones, and flesh of my flesh: she shall be called Woman, because she was taken out of Man. [24]Therefore shall a man leave his father and his mother, and shall cleave unto his wife: and they shall be one flesh. [25]And they were both naked, the man and his wife, and were not ashamed.

Psalm 139:14

I will praise thee; for I am fearfully and wonderfully made: marvelous are thy works; and that my soul knoweth right well.

Acts 17:26

And hath made of one blood all nations of men for to dwell on all the face of the earth, and hath determined the times before appointed, and the bounds of their habitation.

1 Corinthians 15:45–47

[45]And so it is written, The first man Adam was made a living soul; the last Adam was made a quickening spirit. [46]Howbeit that was not first which is spiritual, but that which is natural; and afterward that which is spiritual. [47]The first man is of the earth, earthy: the second man is the Lord from heaven.

During the month of February we celebrate Black History Month. Once, we only had Black History Week. Despite this annual celebration, there is a great amount of black history still unknown and unrecognized in America. We would need a whole year to celebrate Black history, if African Americans were truly recognized for their accomplishments and contributions to America. This is also true of biblical black history. There is a lot of black history in the Bible. Black people played a significant role in God's unfolding redemptive plan.

The First Adam

We will never appreciate who we are until we realize where we came from. Our roots are where the beginning is. Recent articles in notable magazines and newspapers such as, *National Geographic, Times, Newsweek* and *US News and World Report*, indicate that the first human was of African origin and that all languages originated from Africa. Science and the Bible agree on the

> *We will never appreciate who we are until we realize where we came from.*

approximate location, color and diet of the first man. Science and the Bible also agree that all languages developed from one language (see Genesis 11:1–9).

Black history began in the Garden of Eden when God made the first man, Adam. The name Adam is often translated "red man." Many believe that Adam was the color of the fertile soil he was made from, which was black. Many scholars now believe that he resembled a dark Eastern Indian whose skin tone ranges from dark reddish brown to black. It is imperative that we know the color of the first man because according to Acts 17:26, by the blood of one man, God made all nations. Again, it is a genetic fact that only a dark race can make a variety of colors. Therefore, the first Adam had to be a man of dark color.

The Garden of Eden's location, climate as well as Adam and Eve's diet indicate they were dark colored people. Science has proven that climate, diet and environment affects skin color and other physical characteristics. *The Encyclopedia Americana* describes the Garden of Eden as a tropical paradise with its primary source of water being a river that flowed as an underground spring through the garden. The King James Bible mentioned two countries near the garden, Egypt and Ethiopia. Both of these countries are located where the oldest fossils were found according to the November 1985 issue of *National Geographic*. Egypt and Ethiopia are considered to be black nations. This land is often referred to as the land of Ham or Cush.

> *According to Acts 17:26, by the blood of one man, God made all nations. Again, it is a genetic fact that only a dark race can make a variety of colors. Therefore, the first Adam had to be a man of dark color.*

God not only made man and woman in His own image, but He formed man with His own hands, breathed life into him and made him a living soul. The Bible tells us that Adam and Eve were in the garden naked and not ashamed. If we were publicly naked today, we would be ashamed, just as Adam and

Eve were after eating from the tree God had forbidden them to eat from. Why were they not ashamed until after eating from the forbidden tree? God made a divine moral man who was free from sin. When Adam and Eve ate of the tree of the knowledge of good and evil, they sinned. They lost their innocence and became ashamed of what God intended to be acceptable.

The Last Adam

There is a second Adam. Just as we are like the first Adam, so shall we bear the image of the second Adam. The first Adam was a living soul. The second Adam was a life-giving spirit. The first Adam was unholy. The second Adam was holy. The first Adam was conquered by sin. The second Adam conquered sin. The first Adam died. The second Adam died so that the first Adam could live.

> *The first Adam died. The second Adam died so that the first Adam could live.*

The first Adam messed up. The second Adam cleaned him up. The first Adam was a man of color and so was the second. I am so glad God gave us a second Adam, Jesus Christ, our Lord and Savior.

Paint your own picture and color the second Adam any color you want to color Him. John gave us a description of Him in Revelations. John said He looked like an old black man, for His head and hair were like wool and white as snow. His eyes were like a flaming fire and His feet were like brass that had been burned in a furnace (Rev. 1:14–15).

It really does not matter what the second Adam looked like because the Bible says that one day we too will look like Him. Thank God for the second Adam—Jesus Christ.

Christ-Centered Lessons from Adam

What Christ-centered lessons should we learn from this biblical black character, Adam? First, we learn that life is valuable and should be valued. When God breathed life into man, He made man special and placed him above every creature. God did not breathe life into any other animal. He only breathed life into one of His creations and that was man. If we realize that history began when the Lord God breathed life into the very first man who was a man of color, we would not have as much black-on-black crime, suicide and homicide in our country. Things have gone awry. We have to get rid of the curse of Ham and realize where our origin really began.

> *A woman's body should be valued, especially by men, because a woman is part of man.*

The second thing we learn is that a woman's body should be valued, especially by men, because a woman is part of man. Adam said that Eve was bone of his bone and flesh of his flesh (Gen. 2:23). Paul tells us in the book of Ephesians to love our wives as we love our own bodies (Eph. 5:28).

When a man slaps his wife, he is slapping himself because she is flesh of his flesh and bone of his bone. Only a man who does not know who he is or his own value, would beat up on himself. Our marriages must be valuable to us because God ordained the family unit as the first and most important institution on earth. If we realized that it is valuable, we would not have as many divorces.

Summary

When we understand that our history began when God formed us in His hands, we will praise Him for being fearfully and wonderfully made. God not only formed us with His hands, but He also breathed life into us. We are the only ones He breathed life, His very spirit into. When we realize that God formed us with His own hand and breathed His spirit into us, we will not put crack, marijuana, nicotine or alcohol in our bodies. When we realize that God formed

> *When a man slaps his wife, he is slapping himself because she is flesh of his flesh and bone of his bone.*

us with His hand and breathed His spirit into us, we will not overeat. Instead, we will know that our bodies are temples of the Holy Spirit.

God created us in His image. He created us to be like Him. The color of our skin does not matter. What matters is that we do all we can to live Christ-like lives so we can be His witnesses to a lost and dying world.

FROM HAM TO CANAAN

Genesis 9:18–28

18And the sons of Noah, that went forth of the ark, were Shem, and Ham, and Japheth: and Ham is the father of Canaan. 19These are the three sons of Noah: and of them was the whole earth overspread. 20And Noah began to be an husbandman, and he planted a vineyard: 21And he drank of the wine, and was drunken; and he was uncovered within his tent. 22And Ham, the father of Canaan, saw the nakedness of his father, and told his two brethren without. 23And Shem and Japheth took a garment, and laid it upon both their shoulders, and went backward, and covered the nakedness of their father; and their faces were backward, and they saw not their father's nakedness. 24And Noah awoke from his wine, and knew what his younger son had done unto him. 25And he said, Cursed be Canaan; a servant of servants shall he be unto his brethren. 26And he said, Blessed be the Lord God of Shem; and Canaan shall be his servant. 27God shall enlarge Japheth, and he shall dwell in the tents of Shem; and Canaan shall be his servant. 28And Noah lived after the flood three hundred and fifty years.

After the flood, Noah and his sons, Ham, Shem, and Japheth populated the earth and nations of people were spread all over the earth. Ham represents what we know today as the black race. Shem represents the Semitic people. We know them today as the Jewish race. Japheth represents what we know today as the Caucasian or European race.

Slavery and Ham

For centuries, European Americans used the lie about the curse of Ham to justify slavery. In the curse, Noah said that Canaan would serve Shem and Japheth. Thus, we know that the curse was on Canaan, not Ham. We also know that any enslavement of human beings is wrong. When Jesus died, He set all captives free.

> *Slavery was justified in America with the lie of Ham, but Christ taught us that the sin is of the slaveholder and not the slave.*

Slavery is due to the sin of the slaveholder and not the slave. This is completely the opposite of what we have been told about slavery in America. Slavery was justified in America with the lie of Ham, but Christ taught us that the sin is of the slaveholder and not the slave. When the Israelites were enslaved in Egypt, the Egyptians sinned, not the Israelites. It was Ham's folks enslaving Shem's folks. Who were the sinners? The descendants of Ham.

When Nazi Germany used the Jews as slave labor, which resulted in the Holocaust, the Germans sinned. When Arab Muslims held blacks in slavery, the Arab Muslims sinned. I have yet to figure out how the Nation of Islam in America claims a kinship to Arab Muslims when the Arab Muslims were the first to have slaves. History books tell us that Europe got the idea of slavery from the Arab Muslims. The children of Japheth sinned when white Europeans, the sons of Japheth, enslaved black Africans; the sin was not committed by the children of Ham.

What Did Canaan Do?

In Genesis 9:25, Noah cursed Ham's son, Canaan. The question remains: What did Canaan do? As far as we know, there are only two credible witnesses who know the truth of what happened, one is God and the other is Ham. Noah was not a good witness because he was drunk. The best eyewitness was God. God said that Ham looked on his father's nakedness (Gen. 9:22).

What did it mean to look on your father's nakedness? According to Leviticus 18:7, *your father's nakedness* has nothing to do with nudity or being naked. Shem, Japheth and Ham, had probably seen their father naked for over one hundred years. They probably took baths in the same river. It was probably no big deal to see their father or any other man naked for that matter.

> *According to Leviticus 18:7, your father's nakedness has nothing to do with nudity or being naked.*

When I played football, we didn't have private showers. We all showered together and saw each other naked all the time. Men, especially athletes, are generally comfortable with each other's nakedness. It is no big deal. Admittedly, my illustration is based on African-American Alabama culture and not Hebrew culture. Understanding the culture in which the Scripture is written generally leads to a better interpretation.

So what does the Bible say about the father's nakedness? God wrote about it in the Laws of Leviticus. There, He wrote about many abominations, such as, men sleeping with men and women sleeping with women. What God wrote has to do with sexual intercourse. The Bible uses several terms for sexual intercourse, such as, "knew her," "had not known a man," or "went in to her." Today, we have our own language, such as "they made love" or "he slept with her."

> Father's nakedness described sexual intercourse.

Father's nakedness described "sexual intercourse." Leviticus 20:11 says:

> "And the man that lieth with his father's wife hath uncovered his father's nakedness: both of them shall surely be put to death; their blood shall be upon them."

According to this Scripture, when a son had sex with his father's wife, he uncovered his father's nakedness. Deuteronomy 27:20 says, "Cursed be he that lieth with his father's wife; because he uncovereth his father's skirt. And all the people shall say, Amen."

But how is this so? Remember, in the previous chapter, I talked about Adam and Eve, and that Eve was pulled from Adam's rib, and Adam declared that Eve was flesh of his flesh and bone of his bone. Eve's body was a part of Adam's body. Paul said in Ephesians 5:33, *"Nevertheless let every one of you in particular so love his wife even as himself; and the wife see that she reverence her husband."* This Scripture tells us that men are to love their wives just as they love their own bodies, which means that the wife's body is a part of the husband's. Therefore, if a man has sex with someone else's wife, then he has uncovered her husband's nakedness.

With this in mind, the question is who had sex with whom? One interpretation explains that Canaan had sex with Noah's wife. How awful! That is why God had to write all these laws. But it is not an unfamiliar thing. In Genesis 19:30–38, Lot's daughters got him drunk and had sex with him. In Genesis 35:22, Jacob's oldest son, Reuben, had sex with Bilhah, his father's concubine. In Genesis 38:1–26, Judah had sex with his daughter-in-law, Tamar. In 1 Corinthians, Paul tells of a man in the church having sex with his father's wife. Today, there are many records in the courthouse that are filled with cases of incest.

Many theologians and biblical scholars, including my friend, Rev. Dwight McKissic, in whom I have utmost respect, and who wrote the foreword for this book, disagree with the scriptural interpretation that Canaan had sex with his grandmother. Rev. McKissic also refutes Wayne Perryman, who to the best of my knowledge was the first black theologian to disprove the curse of Ham by advocating this same interpretation. McKissic goes on to salute Perryman for his literal approach to Scripture and scholarly work. McKissic concludes, saying that if we can listen to white theologians with similar fallacious and isogetical viewpoints that include homosexual activity, then certainly we can pay attention to Perryman.[4]

McKissic's disagreement is based on the point that the Bible says Ham *"saw his father's nakedness"* and his brothers *"saw not their father's nakedness" (Gen. 9:23)*. The emphasis and ignition of the sin is on the verb *saw* rather than nakedness. There is nothing in the interpretation of Hebrew Scripture that links seeing with a sexual act. Therefore, sexual activity is unrelated to whatever may have happened. Many theologians would believe that the sin that initiated the curse was related to Ham dishonoring his father by not just seeing his father in his condition of being drunk and/or naked, but also making mockery by telling it, as opposed to his brothers who demonstrated honor and respect by covering their father's nakedness and intentionally walking backward in an effort not to see. In Hebrew cultures, disrespect for a parent, especially a father, demanded severe punishment. However, none of this speaks to the point of why Canaan was cursed and Ham was not.

Several interpretations are noteworthy. The noted biblical historian, Josephus said, "...but for Ham, he [Noah] did not curse him, by reason of his nearness in blood, but cursed his posterity."[5] Arthur C. Custance, a white theologian who influenced much of McKissic's research argued:

> What is important to note is that Noah could not pronounce judgment of any kind upon his son, Ham, the actual offender, without passing judgment upon himself, for society held him, the

father, responsible for his son's behavior. To punish Ham, then, he must of necessity pronounce a curse upon Canaan, Ham's son.[6]

Carlisle John Peterson, a black Canadian writer, provides an interesting interpretation of this incident in his book, *The Destiny of the Black Race*:

> Concerning the cursing of Ham...Ham was not cursed, but his son Canaan was. Why was this? We must understand that when the son of man in covenant with God violates his covenantal duty, that son does not experience the consequence of his transgression in his lifetime, but his son experiences the consequences of his father's violation of the covenant. This is not done for the sake of the person who violates the convenant, but for the [name] sake of God's covenant to His covenant-man. When Solomon violated his covenantal duty towards God, the Kingdom was not taken from him, but it was taken from his son.
>
> First Kings 11:11–13 [NKJV} states as follows:
>
> *v.11 Therefore the LORD said to Solomon, "Because you have done this, and have not kept My covenant and My statutes, which I have commanded you, I will surely tear the kingdom away from you and give it to your servant."*

v.12 Nevertheless I will not do it in your days, for the sake of your father David; I will tear it out of the hand of your son.

v.13 However I will not tear away the whole kingdom; I will give one tribe to your son for the sake of My servant David, and for the sake of Jerusalem which I have chosen.

As we see from this passage, the reason Solomon was not punished was for the sake of the covenant God made with David. In the same way, the reason Ham was not cursed was for the sake of the covenant that God made with Noah, so that Noah would not be defamed. Thus, Ham's son was cursed, just as Solomon's son, Rehoboam, was cursed, because of their fathers' violation of the covenant. So Noah passed the curse on to Canaan to punish him convenantally.[7]

Yet, another theory advocates that Noah cursed Canaan as an act of castration because Ham had four sons and Noah had only three. *The New American Commentary* refers to the "No Curse Theory[8]," which espouses that Noah's curse was simply an invocation to God, but there is no evidence that God answered the invocation to curse anybody.

In my opinion, the No Curse Theory should be considered with great caution because it could be interpreted as scholarly justification or undergirding for denying the very existence of the Negro in the Bible. The one good thing about the curse of Ham is that it represents an admission from European theologians that indeed black people are in the Bible. Modern white theologians are now saying as we will discuss in a following section entitled, "From Nimrod to Pentecost" that Ham and Canaan were white and that the black race has no presence in the Bible and has played no part in God's unfolding plan of salvation. Seemingly, the strategy has changed from curse to eliminate. Apparently, the thinking is that since Ham and his descendants have proven to be a great awesome people, most particularly since the bloodline of Jesus can be scripturally traced to the lineage of Ham, let us not curse Ham, but turn him white. In this case, black people should thank God for the unresolved "Curse of Ham" because it indicates and authenticates that we were there. McKissic sums it up this way:

> In Genesis 9:1, it says, 'So God blessed Noah and his sons and said to them: Be frutiful and fill the earth. God blessed Noah and his sons including Ham. To have cursed Ham, God would mean a violation of His covenant with Noah and Noah's sons (Gen. 9:1–17). God remains faithful to his covenant, even when we do not remain faithful. (II Tim. 2:13). Ham was not cursed, Ham was blessed (Gen. 9:1). Ham sinned by showing disrespect for his father, looking upon Noah's nakedness. God in his sovereignty cursed Canaan, not Ham, just as he punished Rehoboam instead of Solomon, out of respect for His covenant. Of Ham's four sons, Canaan, the one who was cursed, no longer exists today as a nation!

We thank God that racist exegetes throughout history have distorted this text for their own selfish purposes. For therein, we can unravel the races of mankind in Scripture. They meant it for our evil, but instead it gave us a compass through biblical trails to discover our presence in the Scripture. This compass leads us to the continent of Africa where we see Ham's sons creating great civilizations, before Europe was civilized. This compass leads us to Mesopotamia (Shinar-Babel) where we see the first world ruler and a mighty man who was a descendant of Ham—Nimrod. This compass leads us to the Nation of Israel being a mixed multitude (Ex. 12:38) having spent many years living in the land of Ham. This compass leads us all the way to to the genealogy of Jesus Christ, where we find four Hamitic ladies in Jesus' family tree. We know the curse of Ham theory was meant for our evil, but God meant it for our good.[9]

As author, preacher, teacher and practitioner of the gospel, I find it both necessary, and troublesome to have to deal with various theological interpretations in this book, which has as one of its primary purposes to lead God's people into a state of revival. It is necessary because the "Curse of Ham" has been used by white Christianity to justify slavery and explain how black people became black, including the negatives that are associated with blackness. It is troublesome because I realize that a theological debate on a subject that cannot be resolved, or on any subject is not in God's formula for revival.

However, there are some things that we can resolve and that will move us forward. First, Ham was not cursed black because his name means black and, in fact, he was indeed not cursed at all, which is evidenced by the earth being ruled and dominated by the descendants of Ham during the first 2000 years of biblical history. Secondly, according to Scripture, Noah, for whatever reason, cursed Canaan, not Ham. Thirdly, regardless of the details of the curse, the curse was conditional. Some evidence of the fulfillment of the curse is shown in Old

> *God does not approve of drunkenness.*

Testament history in that Israel during the Holy Conquest had nothing but success over Canaan. Joshua went over to the promised land, the land of Canaan, fought and won the battle of Jericho, and all those other holy battles, and defeated the Canaanites. Fourthly, and most significantly, all Christians agree that any and all curses were eliminated when Jesus died on the cross.

Christ-Centered Lessons from Ham to Abraham

What are the Christ-centered lessons we are to learn here? First, we learn that slavery is a sin and that the sin is of the slaveholder, not the slave.

Secondly, we learn that God does not approve of drunkenness. To get drunk is a sin. Drinking alcoholic beverages is a dangerous and harmful activity that God does not approve of. Bad things happen when people drink. It does not matter if drinking is done in your home, at a ballpark or on a play-ground, bad things happen when people drink. Over eighty percent of all fatal car accidents in our country are caused by drunk drivers. Drinking and driving is the leading killer in our country, not cancer or high blood pressure. If we stop getting drunk, we will save a whole lot of lives.

Thirdly, we learn that failing to maximize opportunity can be devastating. Noah failed to maximize his opportunity. He had a brand new start, everything was fresh and clean when he stepped out of the boat and into the brink of a brand new day, but he got drunk and laid down in his tent. Mrs. Noah may have been drunk. The Bible doesn't say. Anyway, Mrs. Noah was in the tent with Mr. Noah, and on the brink of a brand new day, when they allowed sin to come in. Fourthly, we are reminded that incest is an abomination to God. Finally, we learn the importance of children honoring and respecting their parents.

Summary

Many may find it difficult to digest the various interpretations of the "curse of Ham," but the important thing is to know that the truth will set us free. The truth is that civilization began in Africa and blacks were present in biblical history. The truth is that Noah cursed Canaan, not Ham and no one is living under a curse now. The truth is God does not want us drunk on wine. In Ephesians 5:18, Paul writes, *"And be not drunk with wine, wherein is excess; but be filled with the Spirit."* The truth is that when God gives us a new start, we ought to maximize the opportunity. Christ has given every believer a new life and we need to make the most of it.

Once we become free, let us not forget who we are and whose we are. God frees us to be all that He intends us to be. He does not liberate us to do every sin we are big enough to do.

FROM CANAAN TO ABRAHAM

Genesis 16:15–16

15And Hagar bare Abram a son: and Abram called his son's name, which Hagar bare, Ishmael. 16And Abram was fourscore and six years old, when Hagar bare Ishmael to Abram.

Genesis 17:1–8

1And when Abram was ninety years old and nine, the Lord appeared to Abram, and said unto him, I am the Almighty God; walk before me, and be thou perfect. 2And I will make my covenant between me and thee, and will multiply thee exceedingly. 3And Abram fell on his face: and God talked with him, saying, 4As for me, behold, my covenant is with thee, and thou shalt be a father of many nations. 5Neither shall thy name any more be called Abram, but thy name shall be Abraham; for a father of many nations have I made thee. 6And I will make thee exceeding fruitful, and I will make nations of thee, and kings shall come out of thee. 7And I will establish my covenant between me and thee and thy seed after thee in their generations for an everlasting covenant, to be a God unto thee, and to thy seed after thee. 8And I will give unto thee, and to thy seed after thee, the land wherein thou art a stranger, all the land of Canaan, for an everlasting possession; and I will be their God.

Romans 4:16

Therefore it is of faith, that it might be by grace; to the end the promise might be sure to all the seed; not to that only which is of the law, but to that also which is of the faith of Abraham; who is the father of us all.

According to the U.S. Department of Commerce and Census Bureau, which determines race in America, if the father or mother is black, regardless of physical features, the child is classified as black. It does not matter what a person looks like, what kind of hair he or she has, or how keen his or her nose may or may not be. If you are wondering what the department founded this upon, apparently they got it right out of the Bible.

Look at the children of Abraham. Abraham had two black wives. One was a black Egyptian, Hagar, and the other was Ketura, a black Canaanite. Neither of their children is considered to be Jews. Ishmael, Hagar's son, had twelve sons. In Genesis 25:16, they are referred to as the twelve princes of their nation. After Sarah's death, Abraham married a second black wife, Ketura, Canaan's daughter. Ketura's name means "pleasantly fragranced."

> *Abraham had two black wives. One was a black Egyptian, Hagar, and the other was Ketura, a black Canaanite. Neither of their children is considered to be Jews.*

She and Abraham had six sons, including one called Midian. Moses' father-in-law, Jethro, was a Midianite. Jethro was the one who established the first court and trial system for Moses and the Israelites. So Ishmael and Midian were half-brothers. Both had a Jewish father, Abraham; yet, neither of them were considered Jewish.

The Canaanite people of Palestine are now known as the Palestinians. They are the Negroes of the Middle East today. If someone were to remove the turban from Arafat's head, put him in a three-piece suit and sit him in an African-American congregation, nobody would look at him strangely.

Who Are Your People?

Black America, as a race, will never appreciate and respect the authority in the Bible until we become familiar with our biblical ancestors and the places where we lived. The following is a dialogue describing who our people are. This conversation could have occurred between two people meeting for the first time, ten thousand years ago. The characters are Henry the Hittite and the Stranger.

The Stranger: "Who are your people?"

Henry the Hittite: "My people are the Hittites. You may have heard of Uriah the Hittite. He's my cousin."

The Stranger: "Oh yeah, I knew Uriah the Hittite. He married a fine girl from Sheba. Her name was Bathsheba."

Henry the Hittite: "You know, Uriah got in trouble a little while back. A distant cousin of his, David, took his old lady and had him killed."

The Stranger: "What? Who is David?"

Henry the Hittite: Oh, you know David. He was King of the Israelites. His grandmother was Ruth, a Moabite, and his great grandmother was Rahab, a Canaanite. But things worked out pretty good for David and Bathsheba. They had a baby. The baby looked like David. He was a light-skinned dude named Solomon.

1,000

He became king also. He had seven hundred concubines and three hundred wives. But there was one wife he favored over the others, a black woman from the Shulamite tribe. He wrote a whole book about her called the Song of Solomon. She was black and beautiful!

The following is another dialogue of "*Who are Your People?*" This conversation is one we might have today and it is nearly the same as ten thousand years ago. The characters are Madeup McCalep and the Stranger.

The Stranger: "Where are you from and who are your people?"

Madeup McCalep: "I'm Madeup McCalep. My people are the McCaleps from Alabama. Do you know any McCaleps?"

The Stranger: "Well yeah, I know George McCalep. He's a crazy dude. He was a football player in the late 50s. He married one of those girls from Tony. It was a whole tribe of them called the Tonyites."

These dialogues show that just as we have this type of conversation today, ten thousand years ago people discussed the same things. The point is that we need to know our ancestors. We need to know where they lived and who they married.

The Importance of Knowing Your People

Why is it important for us to know our ancestors? It is important because we cannot truly be free to accept who we are until we know where we come from and who our people are. Our heritage is defined in our roots. As we look at our biblical black heritage, we learn that black people have always been a significant part of God's plan from the very beginning. As a people, we should find identity, comfort and strength in knowing that God included us when He formed the earth. He included us when He made the first man. He included us when He repopulated the earth after the great flood. And He included us in His covenant with Abraham.

God's plan was for Abraham to be the father of many nations. Interestingly, God changed Abram's name (meaning "exalted father") to Abraham (meaning "father of many nations") only after he married Ketura, the black Canaanite woman, and had a child by her (Gen. 17:1–8). When the child reached age thirteen, God added "ham" to Abram's name and told him that his descendants would be

> God changed Abram's name (meaning "exalted father") to Abraham (meaning "father of many nations") only after he married Ketura, the black Canaanite woman, and had a child by her.

kings and queens of many nations. The name change included the descendants of Ham in the covenant God made with Abraham (Is. 11:1). Including all of Abraham's children in the covenant is proof that God recognized, accepted and loved the children of Hagar and Ketura.[10] Abraham is the father of

Christianity, Judaism and Islam. But God's plan included much more. God's plan of salvation to reconcile man into a right relationship with Him included Christ's tearing down every wall of separation to make one faith, one Spirit, one baptism, and one church. If we believe in Jesus Christ as our personal Savior, then we are members of the body of Christ. We are no longer foreigners. We are no longer slaves to sin. We are God's children.

Christ-Centered Lessons from Abraham

What do we learn from Abraham? First, we learn that God is a promise-keeper. Abram was seventy-five years old when God first appeared to him and made a covenant, promising to make him a great nation (Gen. 12:1–4). Abraham was a hundred years old when Isaac was born (Gen. 21:5). Just because it took twenty-five years does not mean that God ever changed His mind. In that time, He blessed Abraham and in His time He fulfilled His promise.

Secondly, we learn that black people have a rich and significant heritage in the Bible. Unlike America, God did not overlook His children of color. We were present when He created Adam and we were present after the flood. We were present during Abraham's days and our presence is recorded through Revelations.

Finally, we learn that God provides for all of His people. His plan for salvation is for everyone—Jew, Black, Arab, European, Asian, red, black, brown, yellow and white. God said to witness to *"all nations, baptizing them in the name of the Father, and of the Son, and of the Holy Ghost"* (Matt. 28:19).

Summary

Knowing the history of our people is crucial to knowing and accepting ourselves. It is critically important for black people to know that God, the Lord Almighty, the creator of all things, formed us with His own hands, made us black and set us in the middle of His eternal plan. As black people, we need to know who we are and whose we are so we can finally be what God intended us to be.

FROM NIMROD TO
PENTECOST

Genesis 10:6, 8–10

[6]And the sons of Ham; Cush, and Mizraim, and Phut, and Canaan. [8]And Cush begat Nimrod: he began to be a mighty one in the earth. [9]He was a mighty hunter before the Lord: wherefore it is said, Even as Nimrod the mighty hunter before the Lord. [10]And the beginning of his kingdom was Babel, and Erech, and Accad, and Calneh, in the land of Shinar. [11]Out of that land went forth Asshur, and builded Nineveh, and the city Rehoboth, and Calah, [12]And Resen between Nineveh and Calah: the same is a great city.

Genesis 11:1–9

[1]And the whole earth was of one language, and of one speech. [2]And it came to pass, as they journeyed from the east, that they found a plain in the land of Shinar; and they dwelt there. [3]And they said one to another, Go to, let us make brick, and burn them thoroughly. And they had brick for stone, and slime had they for mortar. [4]And they said, Go to, let us build us a city and a tower, whose top may reach unto heaven; and let us make us a name, lest we be scattered abroad upon the face of the whole earth. [5]And the Lord came down to see the city and the tower, which the children of men builded. [6]And the Lord said, Behold, the people is one, and they have all one language; and this they begin to do: and now nothing will be restrained from them, which they have imagined to do. [7]Go to, let us go down, and there confound their language, that they may not understand one another's speech. [8]So the Lord scattered them abroad from thence upon the face of all the earth: and they left off to build the city. [9]Therefore is the name of it called Babel; because the Lord did there confound the language of all the earth: and from thence did the Lord scatter them abroad upon the face of all the earth.

Acts 2:1–8

[1]And when the day of Pentecost was fully come, they were all with one accord in one place. [2]And suddenly there came a sound from heaven as of a rushing mighty wind, and it filled all the house where they were sitting. [3]And there appeared unto them cloven tongues like as of fire, and it sat upon each of them. [4]And they were all filled with the Holy Ghost, and began to speak with other tongues, as the Spirit gave them utterance. [5]And there were dwelling at Jerusalem Jews, devout men, out of every nation under heaven. [6]Now when this was noised abroad, the multitude came together, and were confounded, because that every man heard them speak in his own language. [7]And they were all amazed and marveled, saying one to another, Behold, are not all these which speak Galileans? [8]And how hear we every man in our own tongue, wherein we were born?

One of the long-standing resources for biblical studies, the *International Standard Bible Encyclopedia*, says this about the table of nations found in Genesis 10:6–20:

> "The sons of Ham are Cush, Phut, Mizraim and Canaan. Except for Canaan whose descendants occupy the eastern coastlands of the Mediterranean, these are generally located in Africa. It is evident that all of the people who can be identified as Africans are Caucasoid. There is no nation mentioned that can be identified anthropologically as Negroid. The Nubians, and for that matter, the Ethiopians, while black skinned, do not fit the anthropological description of Negroid. We can only conclude that the Bible limits its references to the people of the Eastern Mediterranean and adjacent areas. And so far as Africa is concerned, this means Northern Africa and the Nile valley to Nubia."

Whoever wrote this is saying that black people are not in the Bible. They even claim that the black-skinned people are white, and that Northern Africa really is not Africa at all. Northern Africa once was accredited for being a part of Africa. It later became known as Africa-Asia, and is now known as the Middle East. The new word for this land is Euro-Africa.

One of the members of the church where I pastor came to me with a look of frustration and her Bible in her hand. She was frustrated because the annotations of her Bible stated that the Canaanites were white. Not only does her Bible's footnote refer to the Canaanites as white, *Webster's Student Dictionary* defines a Hamite as a "Caucasian of the chief native race of North Africa."

We have been raped of our biblical black heritage. In fact, our whole civilization was stolen many years ago. Evidence of our heritage being stolen could be seen on television when a white man named Tarzan became king of the African jungle. He had a white wife, Jane, and the next creature with any intelligence was a monkey name Cheetah. That is what my age group grew up watching on television. Believe me, young people's minds can be affected by such television programs.

> *We have been raped of our biblical black heritage. In fact, our whole civilization was stolen many years ago. Evidence of our heritage being stolen could be seen on television when a white man named Tarzan became king of the African jungle.*

When I first began to research our biblical black heritage, I was angry to find out that someone would scholastically rape a people of their heritage. It is a shame and a sin. We have been raped of who we are; yet, we are finding our source in God, although others have tried to take Him from us. Amazingly, God has raised up the black church and brought us a very long way.

The Contextual Setting

The geographic setting for our text is Iraq. Modern day Iraq was the biblical land of Mesopotamia. It is between the Euphrates and Tigris rivers. Baghdad is right in the middle. It is considered by many as the cradle of civilization. It is in almost the exact location of the land of Ur where Abraham lived when he was called to go by faith to another land. We know that land as Canaan. The setting of our text is where the great cities of Babylon, Rehoboth and Nineveh were located. Assyria bordered one side and Persia the other.

Saddam Hussein is only the most recent of the tyrants and dictators to rule there. Alexander the Great was the first of the Japheth family tree to rule this land around 400 B.C. Hammurabi ruled it for a number of years. Many are

> *Nimrod was the son of Cush and grandson of Ham.*

familiar with the Hammurabi code, "an eye for an eye and a tooth for a tooth." This code has greatly influenced America's justice system. I did my best to research Hammurabi, but was not successful in finding out a lot about him. I did learn that his name means black (Ham) priest (rabbi).

Tiglath-pileser, an Assyrian king, ruled this land and Nebuchadnezzar, the king of Babylon who took Judah into captivity also ruled it. But the first to rule Mesopotamia was Nimrod.

Who Was Nimrod?

Nimrod was the son of Cush and grandson of Ham. His name means "chief, subdued, mighty." He was a mighty hunter before the Lord whose name became proverbial. In other words, people would say then and even centuries later, "I want to be like Nimrod." It is the same today with the proverbial name of Michael Jordan. Many of our kids say, "I want to be like Mike."

Nimrod was the first and only one to ever lead the whole world. He began his rule in the land of Shinar. Shinar is

> *Nimrod was the first and only one to ever lead the whole world.*

referred to in world history as Sumer. History says that those who were of Shinar, the Sumerians, called themselves the black-headed people. The people were a mighty people, and they ruled for the first two thousand years. Furthermore, Asshur, who is a descendant of Cush, went forth out of the land of Shinar. Asshur is the father of the Assyrians. He established the city and country of Assyria.

Shinar was the starting point of civilization and was occupied predominantly by black people. However, not all of the people were black. At the time, there was only one nation that consisted of all people. They had not yet been scattered abroad. This means that Nimrod was leading Shem and Japheth's people. They were one people traveling together, speaking one language.

Nimrod began the kingdom of Babel, which we now know as Babylon. He was the founder of Babylon and the other cities in the land of Shinar. Nimrod led the people in building the tower of Babel. He and his people made the first brick or mortar. He was also the first imperialist or empire builder and an architectural designer. He not only conquered animals, but he also conquered all the people from Assyria to Persia.

Nimrod's Problem

Nimrod had a problem. Before we criticize Nimrod, we should remember that he is not the only biblical character who had a problem. Abraham had a lying problem. He lied about his wife being his sister. Noah had a drinking problem. He got drunk and passed out in his tent. Sampson had a sex problem. This great man spent too much time in Delilah's house. Solomon had a womanizing problem. This great king had too many wives and too many concubines, and he followed them in worshipping idol gods. David had a lust problem. He couldn't keep his hands off of Bathsheba.

Likewise, Nimrod had a problem. His problem was one of arrogance and pride, which is the same problem that plagues many of us today. Many of us do not have to lead the whole world to be arrogant and prideful. All we need is to be given a supervisory position. We don't even need a lot of people to supervise. We only need to supervise one person. Once while in New Jersey, I asked a young man, "What do you do?" He responded by first pointing his finger at the people he supervised and then he said, "I just tell folks what to do." Nimrod had a problem that resembles ours today—arrogance and pride.

> *Nimrod had a problem. His problem was one of arrogance and pride, the same problem that plagues many of us today.*

Why Did The Tower Have To Fall?

According to Genesis 11:1, the whole earth was of one language. Nimrod was leading the nation, but he got the bighead when the people found a plain in the land of Shinar and decided to build a city and a tower there.

Nimrod and the people built the tower because they wanted to go to heaven. They decided to build this tower and make a name for themselves so they would not be scattered across the face of the earth. A casual look at what Nimrod said looks like he had good motives, but he did not. First of all, he said, *"Let us build us a city and a tower, whose top may reach unto heaven" (Gen. 11:4)*. That was stealing God's glory because we know that we cannot work our way to heaven.

Secondly, he said, *"Let us make us a name" (Gen. 11:4)*. Again, his problem was stealing God's glory because when we do something in our name we give ourselves the glory instead of God.

Thirdly, he said, *"Lest we be scattered abroad upon the face of the whole earth" (Gen. 11:4)*. He wanted to keep all the people together, but God was not pleased with this idea. To keep them from building the tower, God confused their language. He gave the people a variety of languages so that they could not understand each other. This place became known as Babel meaning "confusion of tongues." Babel was later known as Babylon and is now Iraq. So Ham, Shem and Japheth's folks were scattered.

Babel and Pentecost

More than one thousand years of biblical history after Nimrod's Babel experience and after Jesus' crucifixion and resurrection, God demonstrated His power with another use of tongues. Jesus instructed His twelve disciples, who were of the lineage of Ham and Japheth, to go back to Jerusalem and be on one accord. He told them to wait in the upper room until He sent them a comforter and friend, the Holy Spirit.

Men from every nation dwelled in Jerusalem. Every nation that had been scattered abroad during Nimrod's day was there. As the multitude came together, they were confounded because now every man heard someone of another nation speaking in his language. They were all amazed at this miraculous, marvelous act. They were saying one to the other, "Aren't these all Galileans? How is it that every man can hear in the language of his birth?"

In Babel, God confused the language and the people. At Pentecost, God brought the language back together again and caused the people to understand.

Nimrod brought all the people together to build a tower in his name and God confused the language. But when God's people came together on one accord at Pentecost, God miraculously allowed them to understand the language of others. In Babel, God confused the language and the people. At Pentecost, God brought the language back together and caused the people to understand.

Once, when my wife and I were in Glorietta, New Mexico, a Native American man was asked to pray, and he did so in his Navajo Indian language. Remarkably, I understood his prayer. It was one of the most miraculous things that ever happened to me. I never studied Navajo in my life, but I somehow understood what he was saying in my own language, just like the men understood each other on the day of Pentecost. God has unlimited power!

Christ-Centered Lessons from Nimrod to Pentecost

What Christ-centered lessons do we learn here? First, we learn that God does not show favoritism. Galatians 6:7 says, *"Be not deceived; God is not mocked: for whatsoever a man soweth, that shall he also reap."* If we sow good, we will reap good, but if we sow bad, we will reap bad. God punishes sin wherever and whenever it is found. God is an equal opportunity punisher. In God's sight, if we're wrong, we're wrong regardless of race or color. It doesn't matter if we are black, white, red, yellow or brown. In God's sight, when we're wrong, we're wrong.

> *God does not show favoritism. Galatians 6:7 says, "Be not deceived; God is not mocked: for whatsoever a man soweth, that shall he also reap."*

Romans 2:11–12 says, *"For there is no respect of persons with God. For as many as have sinned without law shall also perish without law: and as many as have sinned in the law shall be judged by the law."* This Scripture tells us that even if we have never heard of the law, there is still a spirit of consciousness within us that lets us know right from wrong. It does not matter who we are, but what matters is doing right. We need to be sure we are doing right in all of our endeavors. When in leadership positions, we need to be sure when we open up our mouth, we are saying what is right. God rules above with a hand of power and a heart of love, and if I am right, He will fight my battle.

As a pastor of twenty-four years, I have learned not to worry about a lot of stuff, instead I make sure I do what is right. If I do what is right, God will fight my battles.

The second thing we learn is that pride is a destructive sin. Proverbs 16:18–20 says, *"Pride goeth before destruction, and an haughty spirit before a fall."* We need to flush out all pride because if we don't, there will be destruction in our lives. Nimrod and those who followed him were full of pride. That is why their building had to fall. Destruction comes after pride.

Some of us have been in the church a long time and have developed a little self-righteousness within us. We sit in the pews like we deserve to be there, but we must be careful that our pride doesn't catch up with us. I have an antidote for pride. It is called praise. We can praise the pride out of ourselves. I recommend a daily dosage of praise. We need to praise God regularly to flush out our pride. We take pills for everything else—vitamins, diets and more—why not take a few praise pills to make sure we get rid of pride?

> *Only the power of The Holy Spirit can overcome racism. Man cannot overcome racism with his own twisted intellect.*

Lastly, we learn that only the power of the Holy Spirit can overcome racism. Man cannot overcome racism with his twisted intellect. Ignorance relative to biblical black heritage is the root and core of racism. Unless a weed is pulled up from its root, it will grow up again. In other words, we may put a bandage on racism, such as obtaining voting rights, or passing a bill in the Supreme Court, but unless we get to the root of racism, it will spring up again. It will take the power of the Holy Spirit to tear down the lies we have been told and to facilitate the healing and reconciliation that must occur within God's people.

I find it very interesting that history has divided itself into three dimensions. Generally, each race was given approximately two thousand years to reign and dominate. Ham reigned from about 4000 B.C.–2000 B.C. That means that the black race of Ham dominated the known world politically and culturally for the first two thousand years of world history. Shem reigned from 2000 B.C.–300 B.C. Japheth has reigned from 300 B.C. until this present time. Could it be that Japheth's 2000 years are up? Could we be on the brink of the reign of Jesus Christ? I do not know if it is time for Jesus' second coming, but I do know that it is time for Jesus to reign. Everybody else has had 2000 years and messed up. Now, it is time for the Pentecostal Holy Ghost power to reign!

Summary

Our faith cannot be built on institutional religion, not even on the institution of Christianity. Our faith must be built on the person of Jesus Christ. Our faith cannot be built on annotations at the bottom of our Bibles, biblical commentaries, encyclopedias or dictionaries. Our faith must be in Jesus Christ. I dare not trust an encyclopedia. I dare not trust a dictionary. I dare not trust the annotations at the bottom of the page in my Bible. My hope is built on Jesus Christ and it is on Christ, the Solid Rock, I stand for all other ground is sinking sand.

FROM PHUT TO THE CROSS

Genesis 10:6

And the sons of Ham; Cush, and Mizraim, and Phut, and Canaan.

Acts 11:20–21

[20]And some of them were men of Cyprus and Cyrene, which, when they were come to Antioch, spake unto the Grecians, preaching the Lord Jesus. [21]And the hand of the Lord was with them: and a great number believed, and turned unto the Lord.

Acts 13:1–3

[1]Now there were in the church that was at Antioch certain prophets and teachers; as Barnabas, and Simeon that was called Niger, and Lucius of Cyrene, and Manaen, which had been brought up with Herod the tetrarch, and Saul. [2]As they ministered to the Lord, and fasted, the Holy Ghost said, Separate me Barnabas and Saul for the work whereunto I have called them. [3]And when they had fasted and prayed, and laid their hands on them, they sent them away.

Mark 15:21

And they compel one Simon a Cyrenian, who passed by, coming out of the country, the father of Alexander and Rufus, to bear his cross.

The Greenforest McCalep Christian Academic Center, which is now the second largest privately-owned, African-American academic center in the world, is a part of history. It was founded on the idea of who and whose we are. Some fourteen years ago, God gave me the vision to build a school to teach Christian children Christian principles. I promised the parents of the first students that if they enrolled their children, their children would know who and whose they were. I wanted to make sure the students knew that they were more than children of former slaves and sharecroppers, but also children of kings and queens. I wanted them to know that their history did not begin on a slave ship, but in the Garden of Eden when God made Adam. I wanted them to know that they belonged to God and were made in His almighty image. I wanted them to know that God is their Father, Jesus is their Savior, Friend and Elder Brother, and heaven is their home. I believe it is crucial that Christians, especially African-American Christians, know who they are, where they are, where they are going and to whom they belong.

> *I believe it is crucial that Christians, especially African-American Christians, know who they were, where they are, where they are going and to whom they belong.*

The focal biblical black character in the above text is Phut, the third son of Ham. The Bible does not list Phut's descendants, but we do know that he founded Libya. The original inhabitants of Libya were called Phuttites. *Libya* originally meant "black."[11] The Bible mentions Libya and Phut in several Scriptures. The Greek Septuagint and the Latin Vulgate Bible identify Phut as Libya on four different occasions. Libya is adjacent to and was at one time part of what we now call, Cyrene, which is located on the north coast of Africa. The Cyrenians were often called Phuttites. Simon, the Cyrenian who carried Jesus' cross was a descendant of Phut.

From the beginning, God intended for Christianity to be a religion for all people, including blacks. In Acts 11:20–21, we find Africans witnessing to Greeks. The Scripture tells us that some men of Cyprus and Cyrene came from Antioch and preached the gospel of Jesus Christ to the Grecians. A great number of them believed and gave their lives to Christ.

Additionally, Acts 13:1–3 tells us that at least two black men, Simeon called Niger and Lucius of Cyrene, commissioned and ordained the apostle Paul and Barnabas to go and preach the gospel in Europe. One day, while worshipping and fasting, the Holy Ghost instructed these men to dedicate Barnabas and Paul for a special assignment from God. After more fasting and praying,

> *Additionally, Acts 13:1–3 tells us that at least two black men, Simeon called Niger and Lucius of Cyrene, commissioned and ordained the apostle Paul and Barnabas to go and preach the gospel in Europe.*

they laid hands on Paul and Barnabas. Afterwards, Paul and Barnabas went to Europe to preach the gospel.

Is Judaism a Race Or a Religion?

The Cyrenians were of the Jewish faith. We would refer to them as black Jews today. The Phuttites and Libyans in Cyrene today are black Jews. The Jewish philosopher, Judaeus Philo (40 B.C.–40 A.D.), stated that in his lifetime there were over a million black Jews living in North and Central Africa.

What makes a person Jewish? Being a Jew can be defined both in terms of race and religion. The Semitic people would probably disagree with this and say that it is more of a religion or nation. According to Sammy Davis, Jr. (a black man) and Connie Chung (an Asian woman), both of whom claim to be Jewish, it is a religion. America's discrimination laws define Judaism as a race. If we

> *When we are mis-educated, we have to be de-programmed or de-educated before we can be re-educated.*

apply America's one-drop theory, many of the Jewish characters in the Bible would be black, like Paul, David, Joshua, and yes, even Jesus Christ, all of whom had Hamitic blood in them.

Christ-Centered Lessons: The Mis-Education of the Negro

The mis-education of the Negro is a problem in our country, and particularly, in the church. To be mis-educated is to be uneducated. When we are mis-educated, we have to be de-programmed or de-educated before we can be re-educated.

The mis-education of the Negro causes people to refuse Jesus Christ in the following three areas:

1. Europe took Christianity to Africa and the Bible is the white man's book. This mis-education has caused many black husbands to stay home on Sundays because they believe the Bible is the white man's book. True facts that dispel this mis-education are:

   - Ethiopia is the oldest Christian country on this earth.

   - Genesis 10:15–16 tells us that the first Jebusites came from Canaan, which is black.

   - Genesis 10:6–20 lists thirty biblical nations, all descendants of Ham–a black man.

   - Black people helped evangelize and take the gospel to the European world rather than Europe being the first to take the gospel to Africa, as some claim. At least half of the great Christian fathers who shaped theology before the New Testament were of African origin. Even when I studied the founders of Christianity in a black seminary, we were not told this. Saint Clement, the great writer of Christianity, is from Africa, and Saint Augustine, the father of theology, is from Africa.[12] These men shaped the theology of Christianity and, according to our text, a descendant of Phut helped carry the gospel to the Greeks.

   - Rome was not founded in 750 B.C. Greek cities and states were not established until about 800 B.C. This was long after most of the Christian district had already been formed. The recorded history of the sons of Japheth, the now supposedly Caucasian race that is not mentioned much in the Old Testament, does not begin until 1000 B.C.

- There are only twenty references to Rome in the entire Bible and they are all in the New Testament.

- Greece is mentioned twenty-six times in the Bible with only four references in the Old Testament.

- There are one thousand references to the Hamitic cities, places and people in the Bible, in both the Old and New Testaments.

- Luke is the only European author in the entire Bible who can be classified as a son of Japheth. Most of the biblical writers are Semitic with a whole lot more than one drop of Negro blood. If we apply a three or five-drop theory to them, many will be Negro.

- The King James Version of the Bible was translated primarily by white men in England in the 1600s. Black Ethiopian scholars translated it into their language in the fourth century.[13] For all practical purposes, when we compare the translations, they are not different. The second group of men just copied what the first group of men had already written.

2. The second area of mis-education of the Negro is that Islam is the natural religion of the black man. In Elijah Muhammad's book, *The Message to the Black Man in America*, we find these words:

> "Do not tell me that you have unity and
> peace in the white racist religion called
> Christianity...Many of you sing 'Give

me that old time religion'…Islam is that
old time religion."

Many of our black celebrities and other people have
become a part of the Nation of Islam based on Elijah
Muhammad's teaching that Islam is the natural and
only religion for the black man. Elijah Muhammad, the
modern day architect of the Black Muslim faith in
America, was born in Sandersville, Georgia. His original
name was Elijah Poole. He was the son of a Baptist
preacher. Like many of us, Elijah experienced all of the
injustice and prejudices that white America threw our
way. He converted to Islam and was a major part of the
movement that has gone from one leader to another
with the present one being Louis Farrakhan.

True facts that dispel this mis-education are:

- Christ was born in the first century. Muhammad was
  not born until the fifth.[14]
- We learned from our scriptural text that those from
  Niger and Cyrene were witnesses long before Islam
  came about.[14]
- The Judo-Christian Bible is older than the Qur'an.
  Islam even acknowledges that Muhammad included
  a portion of the Judo-Christian Bible in the Qur'an.[14]
- The spread of Islam was as much political and
  economic as it was spiritual. An Islamic military was
  spread across Asia and Africa. Becoming an Islamic
  Muslim was economically and vocationally feasible
  and the right thing to do at the time. Asia and much

of Africa converted to Islam, not because of spirituality, but because of economics, and possibly fear for their lives.[14]

- According to W.E.B. Du Bois, the Nubians (who had Negroid features) fought against the Arab-Muslim movement and did not win; yet, they held on to their Christianity. The Arab-Muslims enslaved the Nubians because they would not convert to Islam.[14]

3. The third area of mis-education of the Negro is that the word *Negro* is negative and a derogatory label. None of us want to be Negroes anymore. It was good enough for W. E. B. Du Bois and Martin Luther King, Jr., but not for us because we believe it implies that we are less than other races. In our mis-education, we have become ashamed of the word *Negro*. White people helped us in our shame because they changed Negro to negra and nigger. There is nothing inherently negative or derogatory in the word

> *There is nothing inherently negative or derogatory in the word Negro from its etymology, which is the study of words.*

Negro from its etymology, which is the study of words. If we apply America's "One Drop Theory" to Old Testament characters, almost all of them would be Negroes.

According to Dr. John L. Johnson's book, *The Original Names and the Descriptions of God and Jesus*, one of the original names for God was Ni or Niger.[15] The name for God, Ni or Niger, is revealed in the oldest written form of the Bible, which the Negro Egyptians called *The Egyptian Book of Light* or *The Book of the Coming Forth of Day*. Europeans later changed the name to *The Egyptian Book of the Dead*.

Ni was a bottomless unlimited water source from which all things came. This is how the Nile and Niger Rivers got there names. Even today, we can find the word Ni in some of the terms that describe the powerfulness of God: omni-present (all present God), omnipotent (all powerful God), and omniscient (all knowing God). The word *Ni* or *Niger* was so sacred to the Egyptians that misusing it was equivalent to taking the Lord's name in vain.

If we study the Egyptian vows, we will find that the name was changed to Am (meaning "I am") and to Im (meaning "Him"). This is where such names as Elohim or Eloham derived. It is also from where the word *amen* was derived.

Contrary to popular opinion, the etymology of the word Niger is not Latin or European, but originated from African language. There is a country called Niger as well as one called Nigeria.

Potato, Tomato, Negro

I find it very interesting that white people in the south could never say Negro. They would call us colored or negra, but not Negro. White people referred to the schools I attended as colored schools, not Negro schools. In polite company, they would use the term negra, instead of nigger. Could they have known what we are just finding out that if they said Negro they were calling us powerful black people? I don't know, but it is possible.

I remember my daddy in the face of white men in the South who used the term negra. Once, after a white man spoke at my school, my daddy looked him in his face and said, "Can you say potato?" The man said, "Potato." Daddy then asked, "Can you say tomato?" And the man said, "Tomato." Lastly, my daddy said, "Then you ought to be able to say Negro." Negro was good enough for W. E. B. Du Bois, Martin Luther King, Jr., my dad and the Negro Egyptians. Then why isn't it good enough for us? It is not good enough because we have been mis-educated regarding the term *Negro*.

> *I find it very interesting that white people in the south could never say Negro...Could they have known what we are just finding out that if they said Negro they were calling us powerful black people?*

Summary

I am glad to know that if someone should ever call me Niger McCalep, they are actually calling me powerful black McCalep. People can now call me anything they want to, and if someone should forget what to call me, just call me a child of God because that is the only name that really matters. Because of what God did, I now have a new name, "Child of God."

I am also glad that we were represented in Jesus' death in a positive way thanks to Simon of Cyrene who picked up the cross and helped Jesus to Calvary. When Jesus stumbled and fell, God had this dark skinned man, Simon, in the right place.

Simon helped Jesus, but in actuality, Jesus helped Simon. Black Simon carried the cross, but Jesus bore it. Jesus did more for Simon and us than we can ever do for Him. He bled, died and rose again for our good.

FROM THE ETHIOPIAN EUNUCH TO THE PASSOVER

Acts 8:25-39 (NIV)

25When they had testified and proclaimed the word of the Lord, Peter and John returned to Jerusalem, preaching the gospel in many Samaritan villages. 26Now an angel of the Lord said to Philip, "Go south to the road—the desert road—that goes down from Jerusalem to Gaza." 27So he started out, and on his way he met an Ethiopian eunuch, an important official in charge of all the treasury of Candace, queen of the Ethiopians. This man had gone to Jerusalem to worship, 28and on his way home was sitting in his chariot reading the book of Isaiah the prophet. 29The Spirit told Philip, "Go to that chariot and stay near it." 30Then Philip ran up to the chariot and heard the man reading Isaiah the prophet. "Do you understand what you are reading?" Philip asked. 31"How can I," he said, "unless someone explains it to me?" So he invited Philip to come up and sit with him. 32The eunuch was reading this passage of Scripture: "He was led like a sheep to the slaughter, and as a lamb before the shearer is silent, so he did not open his mouth. 33In his humiliation he was deprived of justice. Who can speak of his descendants? For his life was taken from the earth." 34The eunuch asked Philip, "Tell me, please, who is the prophet talking about, himself or someone else?" 35Then Philip began with that very passage of Scripture and told him the good news about Jesus. 36As they traveled along the road, they came to some water and the eunuch said, "Look, here is water. Why shouldn't I be baptized?" 38And he gave orders to stop the chariot. Then both Philip and the eunuch went down into the water and Philip baptized him.[16] 39When they came up out of the water, the Spirit of the Lord suddenly took Philip away, and the eunuch did not see him again, but went on his way rejoicing.

Acts 17:26 (NIV)

From one man he made every nation of men, that they should inhabit the whole earth; and he determined the times set for them and the exact places where they should live.

This is the story of Helen the Hen. Helen the Hen was a beautiful young hen who had it going on in the barnyard, at least she thought so. She kind of resented the other old hens. She even referred to them as old bitties. She figured they didn't know anything about what was going on. One day she got tired of scratching for worms and decided to be adventurous. So she saw a cow eating hay and went over to eat hay with him. But her inquiring mind wouldn't let her stop there. She saw a hog eating some slop from his trough, so she went over and started pecking in the slop trough with him. Finally, Helen the Hen went by the farmer's window one day, cackling along. She heard the farmer's wife saying that the farmer wanted some chicken soup. Well, she went back and told the other hens, "I'm tired of scratching for worms. I'm tired of eating hay and I don't want anymore slop. I want some chicken soup." An old mother hen who had been around for a long time said, "Girlfriend, that's dangerous talk." But Helen the Hen figured this old hen didn't know what she was talking about, so she kept on talking about chicken soup. She said, "If the farmer can have chicken soup, then I can have chicken soup too." The old mother hen kept telling her, "That's dangerous talk." She told Helen, "Two weeks ago the farmer was talking about chicken soup and your girlfriend, Gertrude, disappeared. As a matter of fact, I heard the farmer talking last week about chicken soup and your girlfriend, Caledonia, disappeared. And if you keep on talking about wanting chicken soup, you won't be eating it, you will be the chicken soup." The lesson in this story is that we need to know who we are, where we are and where we are going. Helen the Hen obviously did not know.

Deacon Philip and the Eunuch

In Acts 8:25–39, we find an influential black man who knew who he was and where he was, but needed to find out where he was going. This man was a eunuch, an Ethiopian officer who had been to Jerusalem to worship God. Most likely, he was the treasurer for the Queen of Ethiopia, Candace. He was a highly respected man. He was bilingual and could speak and read Hebrew. If he were in America, we would refer to him as the Secretary of Treasury.

The angel of the Lord instructed Deacon Philip to go to the Gaza strip in Jerusalem. While Philip was traveling, he found the eunuch reading the Bible. The man was reading from the book of Isaiah about one who had been led to the slaughter, yet never said a mumbling word. The angel of God instructed Philip to go near the chariot and sit with the man. Philip asked the eunuch if he understood what he was reading. The eunuch said that he did not because there was no one to help him interpret it. The eunuch wanted to know if Isaiah the prophet was talking about himself or someone else. Through this, Philip was able to share the good news of Jesus Christ with him. After Philip shared the gospel with him, the eunuch believed. They rode off in the chariot and when they came to some water, the eunuch wanted to know what would prevent him from being baptized. There was nothing to prevent him from being baptized so Philip took him down to the water and baptized him. Immediately, the Spirit of the Lord took Philip away and the eunuch went on his way rejoicing.

We need a biblical black history lesson here. The setting here is Africa-Asia. This eunuch gives further evidence that white missionaries did not take Christianity to Africa. Christianity was in Africa long before any white European missionaries arrived. This eunuch knew of one God, Yahweh. He had gone to Jerusalem to celebrate passover and to worship God. On his way home, he found Jesus. This text shows us that those who tell us that white men took Christianity to Africa are lying. Our problem is that we don't know who we are, where we are or where we are going.

> *Those who tell us that white men took Christianity to Africa are lying.*

Who Are We?

We are Americans of African descent. Some of us got dropped off in the Caribbean and others in Virginia and South Carolina. Most of us came from the Gambia River area, from the Ivory Coast, and yes, also from Egypt. We are the Ethiopians and Egyptians of the Bible. We are the black hands that carved the Egyptian pyramids and the minds that designed them. We are the Canaanites. We are the eunuchs riding in chariots. We are the Queen of Sheba and Queen Candace of Ethiopia. We are the strong arms of Simon the Cyrene who carried the cross of Jesus. We are slaves who survived two centuries of bondage on the power and sheer will of God. We are the Cushites.

We are somebody, but we have a problem. We have developed a welfare mentality. We want somebody to give us something. I have tried to find the origin of this problem. Perhaps it has to do with the Freedman Bureau Act established after the Civil War to supposedly give African Americans forty acres and a mule. Today, we have a welfare mentality, thinking America and the world owe us something. Many of us are still looking for that forty acres and a mule. I wouldn't mind taking my forty acres, but they can keep the mule. Until that decision is made, which will more than likely never be, I refuse to sit around waiting for somebody to give me something. We were not created to be that kind of people. We have come too far. We are somebody.

> *We are somebody, but we have a problem. We have developed a welfare mentality. We want somebody to give us something.*

I want to bring our attention to Acts 17:26. The Bible tells us that from one man, God made every nation of men. When I was in college, I was particularly interested in genetics. The whole matter of genetics was interesting to me. As I stated in an earlier chapter, scientifically and genetically, only the dark race is capable of producing people of a variety of colors. White cannot produce black. That is a genetic fact, even today. This being the case, Adam had to be a man of color because by the blood of one man, all nations and races were produced. So we know that being black did not begin with Ham or on a slave ship. Which is wrong—genetics or the Bible? I know my Bible is right and I know that genetics still stands as a scientifically proven fact so they both must be correct.

Where Are We?

We not only need to know who we are, but also where we are. We are in the United States of America, not in Africa. We were once slaves and sharecroppers. Now, we spend $5 billion a year in every area of commerce. We spend $450 million a year on CDs and DVDs. We spend $1.5 billion a year on cold drinks. We buy twenty percent of all airline tickets. We buy forty percent of all whiskey. That is nothing to be proud of, but it is an economic reality. African Americans are an economic force in this country.

> *Adam had to be a man of color because by the blood of one man, all nations and races were produced.*

We are not where we should be, but God has brought us much further than where we use to be. Some of us grew up where there was no running water. Some of us grew up with an outdoor bathroom. Some of us grew up walking a long way to get to the bus stop and then to school, having only one pair of shoes and one pair of patched blue jeans. We should praise God for bringing us from where we were to where we are now.

Where Are We Going?

Now that we know who we are and where we are, the question still remains: Where are we going? We are still moving up the corporate ladder, trying to get a piece of the corporate pie. We are still trying to fulfill the American dream. But there is another destination we should be striving to reach. God is our Father, Jesus is our Savior and heaven is our home. I'm so glad that the grave is not our final resting place, but that glory is on our horizon. We need to know where we are going when we leave this earth. We need to know that we are just passing through earth on our journey to our heavenly home to live with God forever. That is where we are going.

Christ-Centered Lessons from the Ethiopian Eunuch

The first Christ-centered lesson we learn is that to be truly black means to be truly spiritual. Black people who are not spiritually in tune to God will not know what it means to be black. Too many of us allow the media to tell us what it is to be black. We allow gangster rap that calls women whores and Bs to tell us that type of behavior is black. We cannot let television and the mass media define what it means to be black. If we separate the black man from God, we will not only

> *To be truly black means to be truly spiritual.*

destroy his spiritual roots, we will also destroy his identity, pride, family and eventually the whole race. The black man must never allow himself to be separated from God. To do so is like a chicken eating chicken soup. God has uniquely made black people. We cannot afford to become like a ship without a sail.

Our second Christ-centered lesson is that we can know about God and attend worship services every Sunday, and yet still not know where we are going when we die. Remember that the eunuch was a bilingual man who knew of God. He would not have gone to Jerusalem to worship if he did not know of God. He knew who God was, but he didn't know where he was going when he died. There are many today who know of God, and go to worship services regularly, but are in need of a Deacon Philip to sit beside them and tell them the good news of Jesus Christ.

We may know of God and can be worshipping Him, but until we accept Jesus Christ as our personal Savior, we are bound for hell. The Ethiopian eunuch, an influential secretary of the treasury, could read the Bible,

> *We can know about God and attend worship services every Sunday, and yet still not know where we are going when we die.*

but he still did not know where he was going when he died. There are many of us today who read the Bible and worship God, but do not know where we are going when we die.

Summary

We all must do as the eunuch and accept Jesus as our Savior. Only when we accept Jesus Christ as Savior, will we know whose we are and where we are going. The eunuch did not need Jesus for an identity. He knew who he was. He knew that he was an Ethiopian with a good job. He did not need Jesus for social status or prestige. He was a high-ranking official in his country. We can have education without salvation. We can have a job without joy. We can have power without peace. The only one who can, with unconditional love, give us all that we don't have and forgive our sins is Jesus Christ. The eunuch recognized that he could have all of Queen Candace's gold and not really have God.

I believe that the eunuch's great-great-great-grandchildren are meant to be among those mentioned in Psalm 68:31 who will go forth stretching their hands to God in adoration. I believe that his grandchildren are now proudly walking around in corporate America today, but they have yet to stretch their hands to God in praise. When the black man, the burnt-faced, comes forth rejoicing in the land of America, there will be a movement in this country. There will be an unparalleled revival of all God's people.

After the eunuch accepted Jesus Christ as savior and was baptized, he came up out of the water rejoicing. If God has done something for us, then we ought to rejoice. If we have been saved by the blood of Jesus Christ, then we ought to rejoice. The eunuch got saved and rejoiced. When we know where we are going, when we know that heaven is our home, we ought to rejoice.

FROM THE CRADLE TO THE CROSS
Mary Had a Little Lamb and His Fleece Was Not
White As Snow

Matthew 1:1–16 (KJV)

[1]The book of the generation of Jesus Christ, the son of David, the son of Abraham. [2]Abraham begat Isaac; and Isaac begat Jacob; and Jacob begat Judas and his brethren; [3]And Judas begat Phares and Zara of Thamar; and Phares begat Esrom; and Esrom begat Aram; [4]And Aram begat Aminadab; and Aminadab begat Naasson; and Naasson begat Salmon; [5]And Salmon begat Boaz of Rachab; and Boaz begat Obed of Ruth; and Obed begat Jesse; [6]And Jesse begat David the king; and David the king begat Solomon of her that had been the wife of Urias; [7]And Solomon begat Roboam; and Roboam begat Abia; and Abia begat Asa; [8]And Asa begat Josaphat; and Josaphat begat Joram; and Joram begat Ozias; [9]And Ozias begat Joatham; and Joatham begat Achaz; and Achaz begat Ezekias; [10]And Ezekias begat Manasses; and Manasses begat Amon; and Amon begat Josiah; [11]And Josiah begat Jechoniah and his brethren, about the time they were carried away to Babylon: [12]And after they were brought to Babylon, Jechoniah begat Salathiel; and Salathiel begat Zorobabel; [13]And Zorobabel begat Abiud; and Abiud begat Eliakim; and Eliakim begat Azor; [14]And Azor begat Sadoc; and Sadoc begat Achim; and Achim begat Eliud; [15]And Eliud begat Eleazar; and Eleazar begat Matthan; and Matthan begat Jacob; [16]And Jacob begat Joseph the husband of Mary, of whom was born Jesus, who is called Christ.

Luke 1:26–38 (NIV)

[26]In the sixth month, God sent the angel Gabriel to Nazareth, a town in Galilee, [27]to a virgin pledged to be married to a man named Joseph, a descendant of David. The virgin's name was Mary. [28]The angel went to her and said, "Greetings, you who are highly favored! The Lord is with

you." [29]Mary was greatly troubled at his words and wondered what kind of greeting this might be. [30]But the angel said to her, "Do not be afraid, Mary, you have found favor with God. [31]You will be with child and give birth to a son, and you are to give him the name Jesus. [32]He will be great and will be called the Son of the Most High. The Lord God will give him the throne of his father David, [33]and he will reign over the house of Jacob forever; his kingdom will never end." [34]"How will this be," Mary asked the angel, "since I am a virgin?" [35]The angel answered, "The Holy Spirit will come upon you, and the power of the Most High will overshadow you. So the holy one to be born will be called the Son of God. [36]Even Elizabeth your relative is going to have a child in her old age, and she who was said to be barren is in her sixth month. [37]For nothing is impossible with God." [38]"I am the Lord's servant," Mary answered. "May it be to me as you have said." Then the angel left her.

Matthew 1:18–24 (KJV)

[18]Now the birth of Jesus Christ was on this wise: When as his mother Mary was espoused to Joseph, before they came together, she was found with child of the Holy Ghost. [19]Then Joseph her husband, being a just man, and not willing to make her a public example, was minded to put her away privily. [20]But while he thought on these things, behold, the angel of the Lord appeared unto him in a dream, saying, Joseph, thou son of David, fear not to take unto thee Mary thy wife: for that which is conceived in her is of the Holy Ghost. [21]And she shall bring forth a son, and thou shalt call his name JESUS: for he shall save his people from their sins. [22]Now all this was done, that it might be fulfilled which was spoken of the Lord by the prophet, saying, [23]Behold, a virgin shall be with child, and shall bring forth a son, and they shall call his name Emmanuel, which being interpreted is, God with us. [24]Then Joseph being raised from sleep did as the angel of the Lord had bidden him, and took unto him his wife.

Luke 1:45–50 (NIV)

45Blessed is she who has believed that what the Lord has said to her will be accomplished!" 46And Mary said: "My soul glorifies the Lord 47and my spirit rejoices in God my Savior, 48for he has been mindful of the humble state of his servant. From now on all generations will call me blessed, 49for the Mighty One has done great things for me—holy is his name. 50His mercy extends to those who fear him, from generation to generation.

M ost of us are familiar with the nursery rhyme below entitled, "Mary had a little Lamb."

> "Mary had a little lamb.
> Its fleece was white as snow.
> And everywhere that Mary went,
> The lamb was sure to go.
> It followed her to school one day,
> Which was against the rule.
> It made the children laugh and play
> To see a lamb at school."

That is the nursery rhyme, "Mary Had a Little Lamb," but I want to focus on another Mary who had a little lamb, and His name was Jesus Christ, the Lamb of God. John 29:36 says, *"Behold the Lamb of God, which taketh away the sin of the world."*

A Beautiful Black Mother and Her Little Lamb

Mary had a little lamb, but His fleece was not as white as snow. Fleece is the wool that covers a sheep. The fleece of Mary's lamb in the nursery rhyme "Mary Had a Little Lamb" may have been white, but the flesh of the Lamb of God, our Lord and savior, Jesus Christ, was not as white as snow. To hear this may make some think that I am implying that Jesus was a sinner, but I am definitely not. However, I am implying that Jesus was of African descent and a man of color.

Mary, the mother of Jesus, was a descendant of David because of her father Heli. David' s father was Jesse. Jesse's father was Obed, whose mother was Ruth the Moabite from the lineage of Ham. For the record, Joseph and Mary were both from the tribe of Judah and of the house of David, but from separate family lines.

Mary was a young girl who had never had sexual intercourse with a man. She is a good biblical example of a beautiful black mother as well as what we ought to be as people of God. To begin with, she was a virgin. God wants us to stay virgins until we get married. When we fail to do so, 1 John 1:9 says, *"If we confess our sins, he is faithful and just to forgive us our sins, and to cleanse us from all unrighteousness."*

> *Mary, the mother of Jesus, was a descendant of David because of her father Heli. David's father was Jesse. Jesse's father was Obed, whose mother was Ruth the Moabite from the lineage of Ham.*

Mary was engaged to a young man named Joseph. In those days, an engagement was more serious than it is today. Joseph's fiancée, Mary, became pregnant and he was not the father. She conceived a child in her womb by the Holy Ghost. The Bible says that Joseph received a visit from an angel and was obedient to the angel's instructions. So he took Mary to be his wife and they had a baby boy named Jesus.

Mary gave birth to the baby. She accepted God's plans. She could have said that she and Joseph didn't have plans for a baby right now. She could have said that she and Joseph had to get the carpentry business going. She could have said that she had to go back to school. What is God asking us to do in our lives that we are not willing to do? Are we holding out on God thinking that He is going to change His mind? Freedom and happiness comes when we yield to God's will. Yielding to God's will brings peace and rest.

When Jesus was of a certain age, King Herod heard of His birth and was jealous because he knew that Jesus would tear down his kingdom. Herod put out a decree to kill infant boys so Mary and Joseph took baby Jesus and fled to Egypt. They hid Him in Egypt until they received word to go back to Canaan, which we now know as Palestine. I don't think they were stupid enough to try to hide a white baby in a black country.

The Genealogy of Jesus

There are a few things we need to see in the genetic lineage of Jesus and Joseph. First, it is important that we are familiar with Genesis 10. It presents a table of where all nations come from. Secondly, it is important that we familiarize ourselves with Matthew 1:1–18. It summarizes the genealogy of our Lord and Savior Jesus Christ, the son of David, the son of Abraham. Most of us do not care for the King James Version with all the begats, so we don't read it. Many of us can't pronounce the names so we just skip it and go to verse 18 where the virgin Mary becomes pregnant. But we need to go back to the begats, because that is where we find our history. We find the black presence and lineage of our Lord and Savior Jesus Christ in

> *I don't think they were stupid enough to try to hide a white baby in a black country.*

the *begats*. There are three Hamitic women in the genealogy of Jesus Christ: Tamar, Rahab and Bathsheba.

The first beautiful black woman in Jesus' genealogy is Tamar (Thamar). Tamar was a Canaanite. We learn best about her in the book of Genesis. Genesis 38:2 says, *"And Judah saw there a daughter of a certain Canaanite, whose name was Shuah; and he took her, and went in unto her."*

Jacob had twelve sons and one of them was named Judah. Judah's wife Shuah had three boys. When Er became of age, Judah found him a wife, a Canaanite woman name Tamar. The Lord did not like Er, so He slew him which left Tamar without a husband. It was the custom in those days for the brother to take his deceased brother's place in marriage, but Onan did not want to have sexual intercourse with Tamar. Judah, told him to go in to her, so he did, but he spilled his semen on the ground. This disturbed Tamar because it was an insult for a lady not to have a baby, so she plotted a scheme.

Tamar knew that her father-in-law was a man about the town, so she dressed up like a harlot, and with her face covered, she sat by the wayside waiting for him to pass by. Sure enough, Judah came along and made an advance toward her, and then slept with her. Tamar conceived his children, twins. The Bible says that during the birth of her sons, Tamara tied a thread around the hand of the baby she thought was coming out first, but suddenly he pulled back his hand and his brother came first. The first child was named Perez (Phares). Afterwards, the baby with the scarlet thread on his hand came out and was given the name Zerah (Zara). And that is how Judah begat Perez and Zerah of Tamar.

The next beautiful black woman in Jesus' genealogy was Rahab (Rachab). Rahab was the Canaanite prostitute who hid the Israelite spies in her house from the Canaanites. During the battle of Jericho she was instructed by the spies to hang a red scarf out of her window, so she and her family would be spared. Rahab obeyed (Joshua 2). She married an Israelite by the name of Salmon. They conceived Boaz. Boaz married Ruth, Naomi's daughter-in-law. Boaz and Ruth had a son named Obed. Obed had a son who was named Jesse, and Jesse had a son named David. Jesse's son is who we know as King David.

The third black woman in Jesus' genealogy is the beautiful Bathsheba, Solomon's mother. Matthew 1:6 tells us that Jesse begat King David, and King David begat Solomon from Bathsheba, the wife of Uriah. The name Sheba means "black." Bathsheba's first husband, Uriah was a Hittite and the Hittites were of the Hamitic tribe, descendants from Ham, which makes them explicitly black. David and Bathsheba had a child name Solomon. So what color does that make Solomon? Regardless of what color David was, Solomon was black.

Yes, we're talking about Solomon who built the temple of God. Nothing could match Solomon's temple. Nothing could match Solomon's temple then and nothing can match it today except the temple of God, which is Jesus Christ. When we think of Solomon, we think of the wisest and richest man ever. He did not ask for riches. Solomon asked for wisdom and God gave him both wisdom and riches. This is the Solomon who wrote at least two books in the Bible, and the one who said, "I am ruddy and handsome." *Ruddy* means "black." He was saying that he was black and handsome. Solomon was what we would call a hunk today. He was good-looking, smart and rich, but he had a problem. He had too many wives and concubines. Yet, his name and his mother's name are in the genealogy of Jesus Christ. Mary had a little lamb and His flesh was not as white as snow.

The Whitening of Christianity

History has taught us for centuries about the black presence in the Bible. The earliest images of Mary were black. Christ's mother, the black Madonna, has been worshiped throughout Europe since the beginning of Christianity. One of the most sacred icons of the Catholic Church is the black Madonna and her black child in her arms. Over the years, thousands of European pilgrims ritually humbled themselves before the image of the black Madonna and her child. However, today most of the black Madonnas have been replaced by Madonnas with European features. It is no question that she started off black, history tells us that. So what happened?

> The earliest images of Mary were black. Christ's mother, the black Madonna, has been worshiped throughout Europe since the beginning of Christianity.

What happened to Mary may be what happened to the Negro mind. Dr. Suzar Epps calls it "blacked out through whitewash."[17] Our minds have been whitewashed, just like the black mother of Jesus. The black Madonna existed until the reign of Napoleon Bonaparte. Napoleon went throughout

France destroying all black Madonnas. This was the beginning of the destruction of these images. Next, he went to Egypt and tore off the noses of the sculptures in Cairo.[18]

The nose is critical in our history. In Africa today, particularly in that marvelous museum in Cairo, you will find statues of great men with missing noses. While visiting there, I asked our tour guide, "Why are the noses missing from the statues?" His answer was, "They fell and all the noses were knocked off." I sat and thought for a moment. Could it be possible that the noses were clipped off? But why would someone do such a thing? I believe it was done to conceal their Negroid features.

Most of the European Catholic churches have not thrown away the black Madonnas because they are sacred. They understand their sacredness so they have stored them away and replaced them with Madonnas of European features. First was the changing of the features, and then the actual change of the color. Today, there are only two European countries that still worship the black Madonna—Poland and Spain.

> *The great Italian painter, Michelangelo, came along and changed biblical characters with no regard to history.*

Next, the great Italian painter, Michelangelo, came along and changed biblical characters with no regard to history. So the whitening of Jesus Christ continued when Michelangelo ignored history. Once again while visiting the Holy Land, I visited churches and museums. It was very interesting to see how things changed from one chapel to another. In the Chapel of Annanias, all of the apostles were black, but when we went to the Greek Orthodox Church, we found that the same apostles were white.

A Biblical Cover-Up

Like Watergate, and most recently Enron and WorldCom, America has a history of cover-ups and attempted cover-up scenarios that have been well documented. Yet, the greatest of America's cover-ups has not been revealed: the cover-up of the black presence and heritage in the Bible. We have heard a lot about journalists being fired for misrepresenting the truth in their reports. Wall Street, NBC and the *New York Times* have all fired people for this reason. The most interesting case was a journalist who was fired for misquoting President Bush. He wrote some of what Bush said, but omitted two important sentences of Bush's complete statement, and was fired for that reason. As I thought on this, I said to myself, "If the same scrutiny was used as a standard of evaluation for the writers of biblical commentaries, the majority of them would be fired or reprimanded for misrepresenting black history in the Bible.

When looking at history and examining all of its research, it seems evident now that the original Israelites were people of color. So the question to be raised is "How did they get white?" I think that is a legitimate question. After all, blacks have been told that they became black through weak theories that range from the curse of Ham to simply staying out in the sun too long. How did Jews of African descent get white? How did Jesus get white?

History says that in ancient Christianity, Jesus was understood to be black. A coin was developed in 705 A.D. with pictures of the Messiah and the emperor, Justine II on it. The emperor appeared on the front of the coin with straight hair and European features, but on the backside of the coin was what people understood Jesus to look like, a man with Negroid features. The Justine coin is still preserved in some museums today.

> *Our problem with history is that our identity has been lost or stolen and now we are suffering because of it. Our minds have been so whitewashed that we hate ourselves.*

White Europeans knew that Jesus was Negroid before African Americans did. Where I grew up we had a saying, "If you will lie, you will steal, and if you will steal, you will kill." My black Alabama upbringing has stuck with me, so I believe even today that if someone lies about one thing, then he or she will lie about anything. If mankind is capable of lying about Watergate, Enron and WorldCom, then they are also capable of deleting a whole civilization and a heritage from the Bible and would deceive the whole world relative to the image of the Son of God.

Christ-Centered Lessons from Jesus' Genealogy

What lessons do we learn from Jesus' genealogy? The first is that history comes alive when we can identify ourselves in it. Our problem with history is that our identity has been lost or stolen and now we are suffering because of it. Our minds have been so whitewashed that we hate ourselves.

If we do not believe that we have been whitewashed, go to the library and look at the yearbooks of the historical black colleges before 1960. In all of these yearbooks, you will find the majority of the head majorettes and the school queens are what we used to call "light bulbs," meaning they were very light-skinned or "high yellow" as they were also referred to in black culture. At some point, our mind started thinking "white is right, yellow is mellow, if you're brown, stick around, but if you're black, get back."

We have looked at our dark skin and hated it so much that we have overlooked a special blessing that God gave His black children—melanin. Melanin is more than a chemical that relates to skin pigmentation. Here are a few more facts about melanin. Melanin is the chemical key to life itself. Melanin is a key ingredient in DNA and the genes that protect the DNA structure. Inefficient melanin in the exoderm causes defective babies. Melanin causes us not to wrinkle quickly. It is an anti-aging agent for us. For the record, light-skinned black people can sometimes have as much melanin as dark-skinned black people. Advanced studies in melanin threaten any key to white supremacy. As a matter of fact, it may completely reverse all of the theories of white supremacy.

All people have melanin. White people produce less melanin than blacks because their pineal glands calcify more, so they produce less of it. DNA testing done on Egyptian mummies shows that they were full of melanin (despite false studies that say the Egyptians were white). America, especially white America, values melanin so much so that there are now melanin ointments. Melanin injections are now being tested. This suggests to me that perhaps white people have a self-hatred problem, also. If not, then why are they trying to look like us? Bigger lips have become sexier in recent years. Many white people risk getting skin cancer trying to get a tan. Some white women even search for ways to have rounder buttocks. They get excited when they have a bouncing, blue-eyed, curly haired baby boy and their description of the ideal mate is tall, dark and handsome.

God gave us a lot of melanin, but we have messed it up. How? When melanin is combined with drugs it is toxic.[19] Cocaine, crack, and yes marijuana, and any chemical based designer drug combined with melanin is toxic. So blacks get addicted faster, stay addicted longer and suffer greater. Actually, marijuana testing on blacks is unfair because of melanin. Blacks will show up positive on a marijuana test even if they haven't smoked a joint in a long time. Melanin is the key chemical. It is the chemical key to black greatness or black destruction.

> *We have generations of lost identities. People without a history are lost people.*

The problem of self-hatred belongs to us and our children, and it has gotten worst since integration. I was one of the many who stood before barking dogs and marched so our children could go to school with white children. Now, our children go to school not knowing who they are or whose they are. They are confused because we are confused. We have generations of lost identities. People without a history are lost people.

When I look at Jesus' genealogy, I am glad to know who we are and whose we are. We were God's chosen people from the beginning of creation. That is who we are. We belong to God and that is whose we are.

Christ-Centered Lessons from Mother Mary

What Christ-centered lessons should we learn from this biblical black character Mother Mary? First, we learn from Mother Mary how to surrender and be submissive. Mary says in Luke 1:38 (NIV), *"I am the Lord's servant."* Some of us have a problem with the word *servant* because we think of it as a slave. There is a difference between a servant and a slave. A servant can walk off of a job, but a slave cannot. A slave is like a prisoner. The apostle Paul indicated that he was a prisoner (a slave) to the Lord Jesus Christ (Eph. 3:1).

Once I hired some boys to cut my lawn. They walked off of the job and left the lawnmower sitting in the middle of the yard. They walked off of the job because they were servants, not slaves. Mary understood that we have a choice to be a servant to the Lord and she committed her life to being one. What a lesson for the sons and daughters of God to learn from Mary, black and highly favored! We too ought to say to God just as Mary did, *"I am the Lord's servant. May it be to me as you have said" (Luke 1:38).*

Secondly, we learn that motherhood should always be valued as a gift from God (Psalm 127:3). Mary was highly favored of God. *Highly favored* is translated as "full of grace." Protestants use the term *highly favored* and Catholics use the term *full of grace*. When a mother is with child, she is full of grace. What does that mean to us today? It means that abortion is never an option. When a female is pregnant, she is full of grace. When a female is pregnant, regardless of her circumstances, she should not kill her baby or herself. She should go to God and let Him work out her situation. I am not condoning premarital sex, but I am condoning the gift of God—children.

Thirdly, we learn that we do not have to give in to negative expectations from our past. We do not have to succumb to the expectation implied by names with negative meanings. Mary's name is the root name of Miriam and Marie. It actually means "bitterness." God took bitterness and turned it into sweetness and joy. Someone may have told us that we would not amount to

> *We learn that motherhood should always be valued as a gift from God*

anything. Don't give in to that negative expectation. If God is able to turn bitterness into sweetness and joy, then He is also able to turn our burdens into blessings.

Lastly, nothing is impossible for God. According to Luke 1:36, like Abraham's wife Sarah, Elizabeth was barren, but God blessed her with a child from her womb. She wanted to know how this was possible. How could she be pregnant when she was old and barren? How did Mary have a baby when she had never had sex with a man? The answer is: there is nothing impossible for God.

When football teams get behind and need one last desperate chance to win the game, they throw what is called a "Hail Mary" pass. They do this when they know there is no way they can win the game. The most interesting thing is that every now and then, the ball gets tipped up in the air and they actually come back and win the game. Somebody has a desperate situation right now and needs to throw a Hail Mary.

At the age of twenty-one, sitting in my dormitory room in Brewton, Alabama, I was saved. I had never believed in Jesus Christ. I had gone through college claiming to be an atheist. I didn't really know what that meant, but it sounded different. There I was in my room reading about the virgin birth, how Mary, who had not known a man, gave birth to the Savior, Jesus Christ. That was the hour I first believed. I didn't know at the time that Mary was black or that Jesus was a man of color. I didn't have any problem with color because the Holy Spirit came into my heart. As a result, I can accept Jesus in any color. He can be pink, orange, red, white or any color. It does not matter to me because He saved me from hell and I am glad about it.

> *I didn't know at the time that Mary was black or that Jesus was a man of color. I didn't have any problem with color because the Holy Spirit came into my heart. As a result, I can accept Jesus in any color. He can be pink, orange, red, white or any color.*

My salvation testimony is further evidence that nothing is impossible for God. God had me, a professed atheist, reading His Word, alone in my dormitory room without any Christian to witness or interpret the Scripture for me. Then, through the power of His Holy Spirit, He saved my soul and changed my life forever.

Summary

"My soul glorifies the Lord, and my spirit rejoices in God my Savior, for he has been mindful of the humble state of his servant." These are the words of Mary's song in Luke 1:46–48 (NIV). She was saying that God had considered her, black Mary, as highly favored. Mary's song of praise should be our song too, for God has also considered us. He considered us while we were still sinners and unworthy, and showed us His favor.

The Lord has done great things. He personally took me, a motherless child at the age of four and became my mother. He personally took me, a big-headed, ugly duckling according to many, and let me know that I was fearfully and wonderfully made. He took all of us, considered our situations and highly favored us despite our mess ups. We are blessed, highly favored and full of grace.

It does not matter what color we are. If we do not receive Jesus Christ in our hearts, we will lift up our eyes in hell. I am glad to be genetically connected to the genealogy of Jesus. One day, I will meet Jesus face to face. All the black history and all the church going is nothing unless we see Him as He is.

If we want to follow Jesus, then we must be willing to yield our identities to the identity He desires to give us. There are three things we must do when yielding to God:
1. We must yield to His will.
2. We must believe in the impossible just as Mary and Joseph did.

3. We must allow God to change us. Although God created us black, our true identity is not in our blackness. It is in Jesus Christ. We need to identify first and foremost with Jesus as our Lord and Savior. In other words, we need to find our identity, and then we need to give it up. That is what happens when we meet Him at the cross.

CHRIST-CENTERED LESSONS FROM BIBLICAL BLACK WOMEN

---

1 Kings 1:1–4

[1]Now king David was old and stricken in years; and they covered him with clothes, but he gat no heat. [2]Wherefore his servants said unto him, Let there be sought for my Lord the king a young virgin: and let her stand before the king, and let her cherish him, and let her lie in thy bosom, that my Lord the king may get heat. [3]So they sought for a fair damsel throughout all the coasts of Israel, and found Abishag a Shunammite, and brought her to the king. [4]And the damsel was very fair, and cherished the king, and ministered to him: but the king knew her not.

1 Kings 2:12–24

[12]Then sat Solomon upon the throne of David his father; and his kingdom was established greatly. [13]And Adonijah the son of Haggith came to Bathsheba the mother of Solomon. And she said, Comest thou peaceably? And he said, Peaceably. [14]He said moreover, I have somewhat to say unto thee. And she said, Say on. [15]And he said, Thou knowest that the kingdom was mine, and that all Israel set their faces on me, that I should reign: howbeit the kingdom is turned about, and is become my brother's: for it was his from the Lord. [16]And now I ask one petition of thee, deny me not. And she said unto him, Say on. [17]And he said, Speak, I pray thee, unto Solomon the king, (for he will not say thee nay,) that he give me Abishag the Shunammite to wife. [18]And Bathsheba said, Well; I will speak for thee unto the king. [19]Bathsheba therefore went unto king Solomon, to speak unto him for Adonijah. And the king rose up to meet her, and bowed himself unto her, and sat down on his throne, and caused a seat to be set for the king's mother; and she sat on his right hand. [20]Then she said, I desire one small petition of thee; I pray thee, say me not nay. And the king said unto her, Ask on, my mother: for I will not say

thee nay. [21]And she said, Let Abishag the Shunammite be given to Adonijah thy brother to wife. [22]And king Solomon answered and said unto his mother, And why dost thou ask Abishag the Shunammite for Adonijah? ask for him the kingdom also; for he is mine elder brother; even for him, and for Abiathar the priest, and for Joab the son of Zeruiah. [23]Then king Solomon sware by the Lord, saying, God do so to me, and more also, if Adonijah have not spoken this word against his own life. [24]Now therefore, as the Lord liveth, which hath established me, and set me on the throne of David my father, and who hath made me a house, as he promised, Adonijah shall be put to death this day.

Song of Solomon 1:5

I am black, but comely, O ye daughters of Jerusalem, as the tents of Kedar, as the curtains of Solomon.

Song of Solomon 6:8–9, 13

[8]There are threescore queens, and fourscore concubines, and virgins without number. [9]My dove, my undefiled is but one; she is the only one of her mother, she is the choice one of her that bare her. The daughters saw her, and blessed her; yea, the queens and the concubines, and they praised her. [13]Return, return, O Shulamite; return, return, that we may look upon thee. What will ye see in the Shulamite? As it were the company of two armies.

1 Kings 11:1

But king Solomon loved many strange women, together with the daughter of Pharaoh, women of the Moabites, Ammonites, Edomites, Zidonians, and Hittites.

Genesis 3:15 (KJV)

And I will put enmity between thee and the woman and between thy seed and her seed and it shall bruise thy head and thou shall bruise thy heel.

Black women have played a major role in biblical black history. From the womb to the tomb, we find the presence of black women. From the womb of the mother of civilization, Eve, and the womb of Mary the Mother of Jesus, we find black women. Likewise, at the empty tomb of Jesus, we find Mary the Mother of Jesus. Other prominent black women in the Bible include, but are not limited to Abraham's two black wives, Hagar and Ketura; Moses' wife, Zipporah; Rahab named in the genealogy of Jesus; the Queen of Sheba; Queen Candace of Ethiopia; Bathsheba, the Phoenician woman; the Samaritan woman who met Jesus in the New Testament; and Asenath, the African wife of Joseph and the mother of nearly twenty percent of the currently accepted Jewish race through her two sons Manasseh and Ephraim.

Contemporarily speaking, black women have historically been the backbone of the black church. The Women's Liberation Movement was not a black culture issue. White America's biblical interpretation of the submissive wife with all its ramifications differs in theology and practice from black culture. The black woman has always played an influential, prominent role in the home, in the workforce and in the church.

A Representative of Beautiful Black Women of the Bible

This is the story about a very beautiful Shunammite woman, Abishag. It is possible that she is the woman Solomon wrote about in the Song of Solomon. Solomon refers to the Shunammite women in Song of Solomon 1:5 as *"black and beautiful.*" But we first learn of this beautiful black woman, Abishag, in 1 Kings 1:1–4. In this text, we learned that King David was a very old man and could not get heat. His servants encouraged him to find the finest woman in the land to lay with him to give him heat. It is a scientific fact that black people give off more heat than other races. Old David laid with Abishag, but he did not have sexual relations with her, just being close to her helped in his latter days.

Abishag and King Solomon

We find Abishag again in the narrative in 1 Kings 2. By this time, Solomon, David's son, is king. Solomon's half-brother, Adonijah, is a little upset with Solomon for being king, but in his heart he knows that the kingship is rightfully Solomon's because it came from God. Adonijah asked Solomon's mother, Bathsheba, if she would go to Solomon and make a request for him. He told her that he knew that the kingdom did not belong to him and that Solomon had inherited everything. The only thing he asked was that Solomon would allow Abishag to be his wife. He just wanted Abishag and Solomon could have everything else. Abishag must have been one fine sister. Solomon's response may be surprising to many of us, but Solomon in so many words told him that he must have lost his mind and that he might as well be asking for the kingdom. Because of Adonijah's request, Solomon had him put to death. Adonijah lost his life just for asking for Abishag.

Solomon thought so much of Abishag that he had his brother killed. Then he sung and wrote about her in the Song of Solomon. We do not know for sure that this is the same

Shunammite woman when he says, *"You are beautiful and comely."* Solomon describes her beauty very sensuously at times. He even says that although he had many women, she is the finest of them all.

According to 1 Kings 11:1, Solomon had many sexual affairs with women of color. God was very displeased with Solomon for having all of these affairs. However, His displeasure was not because of skin color, but because of differences in religion. The Bible clearly teaches us not to be unequally yoked spiritually when we marry. When our children marry, we

> *When our children marry, we should not be concerned about the color of the person they are marrying, but we should be praying that they are marrying a Christian.*

should not be concerned about the color of the person they are marrying, but we should be praying that they are marrying a Christian.

A Beautiful Black Woman as the Body of Christ

The interpretation of the Song of Solomon is a very interesting one. First of all, biblical scholars throughout the years have always understood these Scriptures to be God singing and making love to the church, His bride. If this is God speaking to Israel, then it is really saying that Israel is black because God calls her black. We do not see this interpretation today. Some would rather Solomon make love to a black woman than to have God call Israel black. If Solomon represents God and Abishag is the bride, the body of Christ, then

God is saying, I love you to His church. God loves His church so much that He gave His very life for Her.

AANS

While God is saying that there is nothing more beautiful than a black woman, black women have developed a problem that affects the entire black community. Dr. Suzar Epps calls it the Acquired Anti-Nappy Syndrome (AANS).[20] We have acquired it. We were not born with it. Black women know what it feels like to have mama pulling the hot comb from the fire across their heads with the grease from the back of her hand. I am not trying to change any hairstyles, and I am surely not trying to tell anyone to stop combing his or her hair, but the truth is that psychological damage has been done to us by AANS. It is an outer manifestation of an inward disease of self-rejection and self-hatred. Why did we allow the name dreadlocks to be given to a certain hairstyle? Think about it, "dreadful locks." Quite frankly, I do not like dreadlocks because I have some of that AANS in my thoughts, but why can't we call them love-locks or joinlocks?

Let us look at the etymology of the word *nappy* or *kinky*. The word nappy is derived from an Egyptian word that means "lock of hair." The word kinky is derived from an African word, *ankh*, the name of the most revered symbol in the Nile Valley. It means "to tie, to be joined, to be together, and to connect." It is where we get our words like ankle, neck, knee, tangle and angle. The question is: Why have we allowed Europeans to persuade us that nappy or kinky hair is bad?

Could it be that nappy is divine and spiritual? After all, nappy has its spiral. Most of God's creations are spiral. Nappy hair spirals out of our hair root. Blood spirals through our arteries and veins. Plants spiral out of the ground. The earth spins and spirals and so does the moon and the sun. We put people into space in orbit because we have learned to take advantage of the spiral. Could spiraling nappy hair be spiritually divine?

Christ-Centered Lessons from Beautiful Black Women

What are we to learn from black women in the Bible? First, we learn that God wants us to have a monogamous relationship with Him. Just as women are to be faithful to one husband, and husbands are to be faithful to one wife, God wants us to remain faithful to Him and Him alone. God is a jealous God. We are to have no other god before Him. Idolatry is sin and must not be condoned or practiced.

Secondly, we learn that God used women of color in a powerful way throughout His unfolding plan of redemption. God used Rahab to hide His people as they prepared to conquer and possess the land He promised them. God used Bathsheba to birth King Solomon who built the first temple for the Lord and wrote a book in the Bible that expresses God's love to His people. God used a peasant girl to deliver a Savior to the world. God is still using women of color to spread His gospel—women such as, Dr. Susan Johnson Cook the first female president of the premier historical Hampton University Ministers' Conference Organist and Choir Guild; Bishop Vashti McKenzie, the first female bishop of the powerful

African Methodist Episcopal (A.M.E.) Church; Rev. Trinette McCray, past president of the American Baptist Convention, and a host of others who are listed, but not limited to those profiled by *Ebony* magazine in an article entitled "The 15 Most Influential African-American Female Ministers" (November, 1997).

Thirdly, we learn a lesson on the power of a seed. God used the seed of women to bruise the head of Satan. The head of anything represents authority. From a practical point, this means we can plant the seed of God (the Word) in good soil to bruise and break any authority Satan may have in our lives.

Summary

Lies hurt. I know the employees at Enron and WorldCom who lost 401k plans are hurting because of deceptive lying, but I am hurting a hundred times more than they are because of the deception and misconstruction of our rich biblical black heritage. Also, the truth hurts. Knowing the truth about our psychological self-rejection and self-hatred as evidenced by the Acquired Anti Nappy Syndrome hurts. However, we must realize the truth will set us free and that hurt and pain is necessary for healing.

> *The head of anything represents authority. From a practical point, this means we can plant the seed of God (the Word) in good soil to bruise and break any authority Satan may have in our lives.*

The black woman is somebody. In Genesis 3:15, God speaks to the devil and says that He will put spiritual warfare between Satan and the seed of a woman, and that from the seed of a woman, Satan's head will be bruised. How amazing! It is amazing because a woman does not have seed. She is the receptor of seed. Yet, when Jesus was born of a black virgin woman, a seed of a woman was used to crush the head of Satan and give us victory over death. God is awesome and a black woman is somebody.

Part II: Christ-Centered Lessons from Biblical Characters

Study and Review Questions

1. What evidence do we have that the curse of Ham is a lie?

   First, we know that Ham's name means "black" so he was already black before Noah cursed anyone. Secondly, we know that Noah did not curse Ham. He cursed Canaan. The curse was that Canaan's descendants would be servants to Shem and Japheth's descendants.

2. How do we know that Christianity was present in Africa before the Europeans supposedly took it there?

   History tells us that Tertullian of Carthage, Saint Clement and Saint Augustine were black men and fathers of Christianity. Also, the story of the Ethiopian eunuch in Acts 8:25–39 gives further evidence that blacks knew God and worshipped Him long before white Europeans arrived in Africa. Find other instances that prove the presence of black Christians in the Bible.

3. How can we best identify people of color in the Bible?

   We can identify people of color in the Bible by their lineage and the places they lived.

4. Who was Nimrod? What Christ-centered lesson(s) do we learn from him?

Nimrod was a son of Cush and grandson of Ham. He was the first and only man to ever lead the whole world. Nimrod led the people to build the Tower of Babel. Because of his arrogance and pride, God confused man's language and scattered the people across the world.

We learn from Nimrod that:

- God is no respecter of persons. He does not show favoritism.
- Pride is a destructive sin.
- Only the power of the Holy Spirit can overcome racism. It took the arrival of the Holy Spirit on Pentecost to bring the language back together in such a way that people could understand the message of the gospel.

5. Why did God destroy the Tower of Babel?

God destroyed the Tower of Babel because Nimrod and his people were stealing God's glory. Also, Nimrod wanted to keep all of the people together in one place, but God was not pleased with this idea. God wanted the people to scatter and replenish the earth.

6. How does the Day of Babel parallel the Day of Pentecost?

On the Day of Babel, God confounded the language and the people. On the Day of Pentecost, God did another miracle with tongues. This time he brought the language back together so the people could understand the gospel.

7. In what parts of Africa are black Jews found? How do you think they came to accept Judaism?

Black Jews are found in Northern Africa. Genesis 10:15–6 tells us that the first Jebusites came from Canaan. Canaan is black.

8. Why is Islam not a natural religion for black people?

The Black Muslim faith as we know it today is a product of Elijah Muhammed, a.k.a. Elijah Poole. The religion is as much political as it is spiritual. The Arab Muslims introduced slavery to Europeans, which ultimately led to blacks being enslaved. As Christians, our roots are found in the Bible and our identity is in Jesus Christ. Our history goes back long before Elijah Muhammad and the Qur'an.

9. How can we attend church and worship God, but still not know where we are going when we die?

We can worship God every Sunday, but if we have not accepted Christ as our personal Savior, then we are headed straight to hell. We need to know that as Christians, we are only passing through earth on our way to our heavenly home where we will see Jesus face to face.

10. What is the significance of the black presence in the genealogy of Jesus?

Jesus' genealogy tells us that people of color were included in God's divine plan from the very beginning. When we identify ourselves with our Lord and Savior, Jesus Christ, we can stop hating ourselves and realize that we are fearfully and wonderfully made. Knowing who we are enables us to know whose we are. The black presence in Jesus' genealogy tells us that we are God's chosen people and that we belong to Him.

Part III:

The Prayer of a Black Man Named Jabez (A Kenite)

LORD, BLESS ME INDEED!

---

1 Chronicles 4:9–10

[9]And Jabez was more honorable than his brethren: and his mother called his name Jabez, saying, Because I bare him with sorrow. [10]And Jabez called on the God of Israel, saying, Oh that thou wouldest bless me indeed, and enlarge my coast, and that thine hand might be with me, and that thou wouldest keep me from evil, that it may not grieve me! And God granted him that which he requested.

Jabez is one of the most interesting characters in the Bible. His name is mentioned at the end of names, nations and tribes. In the first four chapters of 1 Chronicles, we find a whole list of names that God inspired. God listed names one after the other, tribes and nations one after the other, and then He gets to Jabez's name and parks there. He puts a coin in the meter on Jabez, and though little is written, there is much to be said about Him.

Who is Jabez?

Many of us had never heard of Jabez before Bruce Wilkinson's book, *The Prayer of Jabez*. Jabez was not as highly profiled in the Bible as Moses, David, Peter, James, John or Paul. His name is hidden in one of the least read books of the Bible. He lived after the Israelites crossed the Jordan River and after the Holy wars that won them the promised land of Canaan. He probably lived during the time of the Judges. Jabez was of the tribe of Judah, the tribe of praise. He rose to be a notable head of his clan, for he was more honorable than his brothers, although his life did not begin that way.

We find a place named Jabez in 1 Chronicles 2:55. If the place is associated with the man in 1 Chronicles 4:9–10, then he would be a Kenite and probably a scribe. The people of the place Jabez were scribes, doctors and lawyers. If we associate the place with the person, we would know that Jabez was a very smart man of color.

What's In a Name?

Jabez's mother named him Jabez because she bore him in pain. There is a lot in a name. We are not as concerned about the meaning of names now as people were during biblical times; yet, we care enough to not name our daughters Jezebel.

There is a lot in a name. My name, *George*, means "farmer, harvester, fruitful." I am fruitful George. My middle initial, "O," stands for Orman. The name Orman has a long history in my family. My father was George Orman McCalep, Sr. I am George

> *Jabez was a very smart man of color.*

Orman McCalep, Jr. My oldest son is Michael Orman McCalep. My middle son is George Orman McCalep III. My youngest son is Timothy Orman McCalep and my grandson is Christopher Orman McCalep.

I always wanted to know where the name Orman came from in my family, so I asked my dad before he passed. He told me that when he attended the University of Kansas in 1933, the registrar asked him for his middle name. He told the man his name was George McCalep. The man said, "But Boy what is your middle name?" My dad said, "I don't have a middle name." The man said, "Well, you can't get into the University of Kansas, boy, unless you have a middle name." So my dad asked him "Well, what is your name?" The man replied, "My name is John O. Foster." My dad said, "Well that's good enough for me. That is how my dad became George O. McCalep.

My granddaddy began calling my daddy Oscar. I remember my granddaddy introducing me as Oscar's boy. It turned out that my mother's best friend's maiden name was Orman so the family began to associate the "O" with Orman.

Three years ago, when we were in the Greek Isles, tracing the footsteps of Paul. We kept passing a place called Ormand while in the ancient city of Ephesus, which is now the Republic of Turkey. We passed by Ormand Mountain. Finally, I became too curious to contain myself. Other than my family, I had never known an Orman before. So I asked the Turkish guide, "What does the name Ormand mean?" She said, "The name *Ormand* means forest." There was a sudden quietness on the bus. One of the deacons from our church, Deacon Boyd, said to me, "Well, Pastor, you had to come all the way to Ephesus to get confirmation that God appointed you to pastor at Greenforest." My name is George Orman, which means "fruitful forest."

Jabez's name did not have such a positive beginning, for his name meant pain and could also be translated as trouble. The Scripture does not say why his mother experienced sorrow. Perhaps she had a difficult pregnancy, a hard delivery or a generational curse. Still his name meant that he had a hard, difficult beginning, but God has the power to change such beginnings.

The Awesome Power of God

God has the power to help us overcome difficult situations, as well as to break generational curses. It is a bad thing to live together before getting married, but God has the power to sanctify and purify even a marriage with a bad beginning. God has the power to purify a fornicator and restore him or her to righteousness. God has the power to make a bastard child honorable, even among brothers and sisters.

God also has the power to break all generational curses. Just because our fathers and grandfathers were drunks, does not mean we have to be drunks. Just because our brothers and sisters were drug addicts, does not mean we have to be drug addicts. Just because our mothers had lots of children out of wedlock with a lot of different men, does not mean that we have to have lots of children out of wedlock with a lot of different men. Just because most of our family

> *God also has the power to break all generational curses.*

members had broken marriages, does not mean our marriages have to end broken. Just because our fathers were rolling stones, does not mean we have to be womanizers. Just because our parents were child abusers, does not mean that we have to be abusers. God has the power to break all generational curses, including these.

Jabez's Success Secret

Jabez's life began in pain and trouble, but God made him honorable. What was Jabez's secret? Jabez found strength, power and a river of blessings in a simple prayer. He asked God to bless him. Jesus told us to ask and it shall be given unto us. The Bible also tells us that we have not because we ask not. There are many blessings that go unclaimed because we fail to simply ask. Imagine, when we get to heaven, Saint Peter will show us around and take us to see the unclaimed or unasked for blessings with our names on them.

Jabez had the courage, boldness and faith to ask God to bless him, and bless him indeed. *Indeed* means "to really want God to bless us a lot." Jabez was actually asking God to bless him every time the sun came up and went down.

We are not blessed as much as we could be because we simply do not constantly ask. God wants us to constantly ask. Our problem is that we seem to think that God does not have enough blessings. We seem to want

> *We are not blessed as much as we could be because we simply do not constantly ask.*

to limit God's blessing power. We think that because God once blessed us and our neighbors, friends and family, that He is out of blessings. But His blessings are unlimited. We should keep asking Him over and over again to bless us indeed and He will keep blessing us over and over again.

Notice, that Jabez left the what, when, where and how of the blessing entirely in God's hand. He didn't say, "I want a Lexus, Mercedes, new home or wife." He didn't say, "Lord I need this blessing before the sun goes down" or "Send me a fast angel." Many of us want God to bless us and bless us quickly, before the sun goes down. Any way that God chose to bless Jabez was all right with Jabez.

Spiritual Nuggets for Abundant Living

What golden nuggets can we learn here? First, we learn without question that it is not what our parents decide for us or the hand that life deals us that counts the most. Life can sometimes deal us a bad hand. Trouble and pain may be our middle name, but what matters most is realizing what we want to be and asking God for it.

Secondly, we learn that if we do not ask for all the blessings that God has for us, we will only receive those we do not ask for. God has many blessings with our names on them, but the key to receiving all of them is to ask for them. How many times have we been blessed with something we did not ask for? God has blessed me with a lot of

> *It is God's nature to bless.*

things I never asked for. These kinds of blessings are only a fraction of the blessings God has for us, but that is all we will receive until we ask for more. Those who are blessed indeed think differently. Jabez was made honorable among his brothers because of his courage and boldness to think differently.

Thirdly, we learn that it is God's nature to bless. Do not hesitate to ask God to bless you because it is His nature to do so. God is a loving Father who never gets tired of His children asking him for help. He is a blessed God and He is in the blessing business. He blesses us with His kindness, joy, peace, grace, mercy and His unconditional love. Greatest of all, He blessed us with His son, Jesus Christ, who died for our salvation. Jesus blessed us when He died for all the wrong we had ever done and gave us eternal life.

Summary

What we name our children is important because whatever their names mean, we walk around claiming them to be that each time we call their names. Like Jabez, when we have a relationship with God, we have the right to ask Him to change our names or to bless us despite of our names. A relationship with God far exceeds a relationship with others, even our parents, because only God has the power to change our situations and break generational curses.

Jabez found the secret to success was asking God for what he needed and desired. We too have access to Jabez's secret. God granted Jabez's request and He will grant ours too. What He has done for others, He will do for us. Jesus did not come to bless Jabez and a few others. He came to bless all of us with abundant and eternal life. We may be one prayer away so, stay on the prayer line. Just keep asking.

ENLARGE MY COAST, INCREASE MY TERRITORY, AND THAT THINE HAND MIGHT BE WITH ME

---

1 Chronicles 4:9–10

9And Jabez was more honorable than his brethren: and his mother called his name Jabez, saying, Because I bare him with sorrow. 10And Jabez called on the God of Israel, saying, Oh that thou wouldest bless me indeed, and enlarge my coast, and that thine hand might be with me, and that thou wouldest keep me from evil, that it may not grieve me! And God granted him that which he requested.

J abez asked God to expand his territory and increase his coast. He was saying to God, "Give me more opportunities and responsibilities to witness for You and to be more for You." Paul says there are two persons in us, Mr. Flesh and Mr. Spirit. Mr. Flesh does not want his territory expanded because he does not want more responsibility. Mr. Spirit wants his territory expanded because he knows the power of God.

> *Jabez asked God to expand his territory and increase his coast. He was saying to God, "Give me more opportunities and responsibilities to witness for You and to be more for You."*

I too know the power of God. Like Jabez, I once asked God to enlarge my territory and increase my coast. I prayed this prayer and God showed me Greenforest Junior College. Then I thought, "I'm not going to pray that prayer anymore. The way I feel about the responsibility I already have, I don't need any more territory or coast."

Lord, Keep Your Hand Upon Us

Next, Jabez asked God to keep His hand upon him. In other words, he asked God, "Lord, give me strength for the responsibility I'm asking for." He wanted God to protect him from himself after He had blessed him. He did not want to get a bighead. It is easy to get the big head when God blesses us. The old people were always concerned about their children not being too successful before they were mature enough to handle it. I had a college coach like that, Coach George Herman Hobson.

I thought I was the best quarterback on my college campus. Coach Hobson and all the players knew I was the best also, but he would not let me be the starting quarterback. I remember our team playing a game against Morehouse College. We were behind. The game was nearly over when the coach put me in the game. He said, "Mickey get over there, light it up and bring us back." So I jumped off the bench and within four or five minutes, we had scored three or four touchdowns and won the game. After this game, I just knew I would be the starting quarterback, but I was wrong. Coach Hobson sat me right back on the bench. So I asked him, "Coach, why am I not starting?" And he said, "If I let you start, you will be successful, get the bighead and be ruined for the rest of your life." Those words from forty-four years ago still ring. He

> *Jabez asked God to keep His hand upon him. In other words, he asked God, "Lord, give me strength for the responsibility I'm asking for."*

did not say that I would be ruined for a season, but for the rest of my life. So I sat on that hard bench for the rest of the season.

I find it interesting and a good sign that many of our young stars now have their parents managing their money. The parents know that their children are too young for all this stardom. We have seen those who did not trust their parents. They ended up with the bighead and we know the results.

A preacher from Milwaukee visited the Greenforest ministry. He said to me, "Pastor, I see why I'm not blessed." I said, "What do you mean, Reverend?" He said, "Well, I'm going to tell you. You see if I pastored a church the size of Greenforest, nobody could talk to me and I would not talk to anyone." I said to him, "You're kidding." He said, "I'm serious." After going back and forth with him for awhile, I finally understood what he was saying. He was saying that he would have the bighead if he pastored a mega-church. Increase our coast Lord, but keep Your hand upon us.

Spiritual Nuggets for Abundant Living

What golden nuggets can we learn here? First, we learn that if we attempt great things for God, we can expect great things from Him. The problem is that we do not attempt great things for God. Our efforts are too frail, our visions are too small, our dreams are too little, our expectations are too limited or too low and our attempts are too seldom. Our attempts should be

> *If we attempt great things for God, we can expect great things from Him.*

often and our expectations should be high. We need to turn our seldom attempts and low expectations into frequent attempts and high expectations. If we constantly attempt great things for God, we can expect great things from Him. Why? Because we can't beat God giving, and it pays to serve Jesus Christ.

Secondly, we learn that God's return will always be greater than the service we render. We cannot beat God's goodness. God is good all the time and all the time God is good. We cannot do more for God than He will do for us.

Everybody ought to have a human friend like God, but not all of us do. I have only had one in my lifetime. I have a friend who worked with me at Georgia State University, Dr. Charlie Exsley. He attended my installation service at Greenforest as well as other significant events in my life. I cannot out give Charlie in our relationship. I have tried, but he just keeps out giving me. Everybody ought to have a friend like Charlie.

Thirdly, we learn that we cannot do and be more for God without Him blessing us materially. Jabez did not ask for material things. As a matter of fact, he really did not ask God for anything. Yet, he asked Him for everything. He only asked if God would expand his territory and enlarge his coast. He asked God for more opportunities and responsibilities. Jabez was simply asking God if He could be and do more for Him.

I have discovered that we cannot do more and be more for God without Him blessing us materially. I would like to make an addendum to Jabez's prayer. You may call it "McCalep's Discovery." I have discovered that God does not expand our coast without expanding our pocketbook. I have discovered that God does not enlarge our territory without enlarging our paycheck. That is why whatever He does for us, we need to ask Him to keep His hand upon us. Whatever God blesses us with, we need to use it to bless somebody else so we can expand His kingdom, which is part of His divine plan.

> *God's return will always be greater than the service we render.*

Summary

We need to ask God to bless us indeed. We also need to ask God to enlarge our territory, to give us more opportunities and responsibilities. But we cannot conclude Jabez's prayer there. We need to continue Jabez's prayer and ask God to keep His hands upon us so we do not sin, but remain committed to the opportunities and responsibilities we asked Him for.

It pays every step of the way to serve Jesus Christ. Although the pathway of glory may sometimes be dreary, we will be happy in the end. We may not be happy every step, but we will have joy on our journey. Joy is that everlasting peace that comes from being in a right relationship with God. If we do not have joy in this Christian journey, something is wrong with our lives. Continue to pray Jabez's prayer until you get it in your heart. Then, expect great things from God.

KEEP ME FROM EVIL THAT IT MAY NOT GRIEVE ME

---

1 Chronicles 4:9–10

[9]And Jabez was more honorable than his brethren: and his mother called his name Jabez, saying, Because I bare him with sorrow. [10]And Jabez called on the God of Israel, saying, Oh that thou wouldest bless me indeed, and enlarge my coast, and that thine hand might be with me, and that thou wouldest keep me from evil, that it may not grieve me! And God granted him that which he requested.

Jabez prayed that God would keep him from evil. He was actually praying for God to protect his mind and eyes from being tempted. He was simply asking God not to let him read or see anything that might cause him to sin. We all have weak days. The devil will put something pretty in our path at our weakest moment. He will put a pretty woman on the elevator wearing a body shirt that reveals most of her breasts. The devil knows how to package sin. He is the great marketer of it.

A story is told of a Christian man who got on an elevator and the devil placed a woman wearing a short, tight skirt right in front of him. When the man got off the elevator, he was so upset and confused that he tried to pray the Twenty-third Psalm. His version of the Psalm began something like this, "The Lord is my shepherd and I see what I want." He was trying to ask God to keep him from evil, but was having a hard time resisting the temptation set before him.

> *Jabez prayed that God would keep him from evil. He was actually praying for God to protect his mind and eyes from being tempted.*

Jabez realized that temptation causes sin. For that reason, we need to pray constantly. We need to ask God to keep us from watching evil whether evil is presented live, on television, in a magazine or on the Internet.

We also need to ask God to keep us from participating in evil, such as fights and gossip. When God keeps us from evil, we will not want anybody calling us on the phone to tell us something bad about somebody else. Some of us sit by the phone hoping someone will call us with gossip. Jabez prayed that evil would not come into his path. He wanted to stay out of fights. The best way not to lose a fight is to ask God to keep us out of one.

Sin Is Destructive

Jabez realized that sin causes pain and is destructive. He knew that sin would cut off his blessings. Sinning is like cutting off our electricity. Jabez did not want to cause or receive pain in any form. That is why he prayed, *"That it may not grieve me!"*

I would like to use an adulterous relationship as an illustration. I do not care how pleasurable or discreet, or how many consenting adults are involved, an adulterous relationship always hurts someone. It may be the husband, the wife, the other person or even the children, but in an adulterous relationship, someone always gets hurt. Sin causes pain, and the best way not to cause pain or grief is to depend on God to keep evil and temptation from us.

> *Sin causes pain, and the best way not to cause pain or grief is to depend on God to keep evil and temptation from us.*

Letting Go of Our Painful Past

We must also pray that God will remove pain from our past. Again, Jabez's name means pain, sorrow or trouble. He had a painful past. We have to deal with the pain of our past. I find it interesting that there is a class at my church for women dealing with pain, but there is not one for men, as though we men do not have pain in our past. We men have as much pain in our past as women have in theirs.

Once on a plane to California, I picked up a brochure and began reading about some of the places and sites in California, and started to cry. I cried because I remembered when I was

> *Past pain affects our current relationships.*

twelve years old and did not get to go to California to the National Boy Scout Jamboree. I will never forget it. Every boy in my group and neighborhood got to go, but my dad would not let me go unless I earned enough money. I cut all the grass and chopped all the wood I could, but I still came up short. When you came up short with my dad, you were just short. I remember all the other kids catching the train to California. Years later, as a grown man, on my way to California, I still remembered the pain and hurt.

We all need and have to deal with pain. When we don't, it does not go away; it is just suppressed. If we are going to be all that we can be for God, then we have to deal with the pain of our past.

Spiritual Nuggets for Abundant Living

What golden nuggets can we learn here? First we learn that past pain affects our current relationships. It affects our relationship with God, His people and all people. Past pain even affects our parenting and our marriages. Many of us do not have good marriage relationships because we are still dealing with the pain of our past. The best way to deal with past pain is to pray for God to take it away from us. Pain of generational curses, e.g., alcoholism, drug addiction, divorces and abusiveness in the family, lingers with many of us, but we have to deal with it. How did Jabez deal with pain? He prayed for God to protect him from it so he would not be grieved or receive pain.

Past pain even affects one's pastorate. I can remember the most hurtful situation I ever had over the twenty-four years I have been a pastor. I was in a church meeting where something very painful to me was being discussed so I asked to be excused. I remember the chairman of the meeting asking me what was wrong. I told him that I would be back when they finished talking about a particular subject. Then, I shared my pain with the group. The chairman told the committee to stop and pray for me, the pastor, right then so that God would remove my pain. They stopped the discussion, gathered around me, and then while laying hands on me, the committee prayed and God took my pain away.

Secondly, we learn that we need to focus less on beating temptations and more on avoiding them. We tend to want to beat the devil when we can avoid him in many cases. There is a Mountain Dew commercial where a boy is butting heads with a billy goat because the

> *We need to focus less on beating temptations and more on avoiding them.*

billy goat has his Mountain Dew. I don't care how much Mountain Dew we drink, we cannot out butt a billy goat. Satan is the billy goat that we keep trying to out butt. We cannot win in Satan's territory playing with his weapons, yet that is exactly what we try to do. Somebody is going to enter into a butting contest with a billy goat on his or her job tomorrow. The best way not to lose the fight is not to get in it.

Thirdly, we learn that when God does not keep us from temptation, He will give us the power to overcome evil. When we find ourselves in spiritual warfare that we cannot avoid, we need to know that God can and will deliver us. There are times when we should launch an offensive attack against evil. We have at least one offensive weapon in our spiritual armor and that is the sword of the Spirit—the Word of God. Our sword can be sharpened with praise, prayer and meditation. When we find ourselves in a fight that we cannot get out of and when we have done all we can in using our offensive weapons, we should just stand because God can and will deliver us.

> *Depending on God makes honorable people out of ordinary people.*

Fourthly, we learn that depending on God makes honorable people out of ordinary people. Jabez was honorable among all his brethren because he depended on God. Depending on God means putting God's agenda before ours before we go for the gusto. When we go for the gusto, we attempt to do something large enough to guarantee failure, unless God steps in.

The church I pastor has a vision that is much bigger than us, big enough to guarantee failure. The vision is big enough that I know we cannot do it. It guarantees failure. That is what happens when we go for the gusto and depend on God. It means going out on the limb far enough that we know the only way it can happen is if God shows up. There is a God who rules above with a hand of power and a heart of love, who will fight our battles according to His Word and His will. There is power in depending on God. Jabez called on God and depended on Him.

Summary

The more God blesses us, the more the devil will tempt us. The more God blesses us, the more the devil will repackage sin. If Satan's first commercial does not get us, he will repackage it and make a prettier one for his next move on us. We must ask God to keep His hands upon us so we do not experience the unnecessary pain caused by sin.

THE BOOKENDS OF JABEZ'S PRAYER
(Why God Answered Jabez's Prayer)

1 Chronicles 4:9–10

9And Jabez was more honorable than his brethren: and his mother called his name Jabez, saying, Because I bare him with sorrow. 10And Jabez called on the God of Israel, saying, Oh that thou wouldest bless me indeed, and enlarge my coast, and that thine hand might be with me, and that thou wouldest keep me from evil, that it may not grieve me! And God granted him that which he requested.

The first and last lines of Jabez's petition are of the utmost importance. The first line of his prayer says, "And Jabez called on the God of Israel." The last line says, "And God granted him that which he requested." I thank God for His Holy Spirit revealing the bookends of Jabez's prayer to me so I can share them with others.

Why Did God Grant Jabez's Request?

Why did God answer Jabez's prayer? I think we can find the answer as we look at this first part of the bookends. The first thing we know about Jabez is that he was a praying man. Jabez prayed to the God of Israel.

> *God granted Jabez his prayer request because he prayed to the right God.*

It is good to associate with praying people. I am thankful that I married a praying woman. My wife never leaves home without going to her prayer room and praying first. Maybe that is why she has been able to put up with me for over forty years. The Bible tells us that it is a good thing for a man to find a wife. I say that a man finds an even better thing when he finds a praying wife.

God granted Jabez his prayer request because he prayed to the right God, the God of Israel. The God of Israel, in the Old Testament, is the same God in the New Testament to whom we say "our Father." The Father and the Son are one. That is why it is important to pray in the name of Jesus. Be sure to pray in the right name because there are a lot of little "g" gods. The Bible tells us that whatever we ask, to ask it in Jesus' name. Why? There is power in the name of Jesus. God answered Jabez's prayer not only because he prayed, but also because he prayed to the right God.

Another reason God answered Jabez's prayer was because he prayed with the right motives. Jabez prayed a sincere prayer. God warns us in Matthew 6:5 about praying like hypocrites. The word *hypocrite* means "to pray with the wrong motive." I have never known of anyone in the church to admit to being a hypocrite. People will sometimes admit to being a drunk, drug addict or even sleeping around, but never a hypocrite. God tells us to be careful that we do not pray with the wrong motives like the hypocrites. God answered Jabez's prayer because he prayed, he prayed to the right God and he prayed with the right motives.

The fourth reason God granted Jabez's prayer is because he prayed a righteous prayer. Jabez submitted a righteous petition: *"Oh, that you would bless me and enlarge my territory! Let your hand be with me, and keep me from harm so that I will be free from pain"* (1 Chron. 4:10 NIV). This is a righteous prayer because its goal is to fulfill the purposes of God. God has told us in and through His Son, Jesus Christ, to seek first His kingdom and His righteousness, and all other things will be added unto us (Matt. 6:33). God granted Jabez's prayer because he prayed, he prayed to the right God, he prayed with the right motives and he prayed a righteous prayer.

"And God granted him that which he requested" (1 Chron. 4:10). God wants to hear our prayers. The problem is that we have not internalized and spiritualized that in our hearts. God is graciously sitting on heaven's throne longing to

hear from us. He is sitting by the phone expecting a call. It is like what happens after a good job interview: the interviewer promises to call, so we wait by the phone anxiously waiting to hear from him or her; or it is like giving our phone number to a very attractive person so we sit by the phone waiting to hear from him or her. God is a gracious God who is sitting on heaven's throne longing to hear from us.

Our problem is that we simply do not pray. The admonition is not necessarily to pray Jabez's prayer, but simply to pray. One of the most positive things about Jabez's prayer is that it has caused people to pray who never prayed before. The popularity of Jabez's prayer has caused people to talk to God who have never talked to Him before.

> *Our problem is that we simply do not pray. The admonition is not necessarily to pray Jabez's prayer, but simply to pray.*

God did not just start wanting to hear from us. He has been longing to hear from us since our very existence. He has always urged men and women to pray. He told us to pray without ceasing in 1 Thessalonians 5:17. He did not say, "if we pray" but, "when we pray." He has said that everybody ought to pray.

How Has God Taught Us To Pray?

There are several biblical models of prayer. We could look at the prayer that Jesus taught the disciples to pray, the Lord's Prayer (Matt. 6:9–13). We could also look at Paul's prayers in the book of Ephesians (Eph. 1:16–23, 3:14–21). We can pray the prayer of Jabez, the Lord's Prayer, Paul's prayers or our own prayer.

In my book, *How to be Blessed*, there is a chapter about being blessed through prayer and fasting. I challenge the reader to take the "McCalep How to be Blessed Test" for three weeks—three weeks of fasting while praying one of the three prayers mentioned in the book. Using one of these three prayers guarantees that the person will not be praying amiss because he or she will be praying a model biblical prayer.

We often pray amiss because we do not pray within God's will. We pray amiss because we pray selfishly. Our prayers are amiss because if a yes answer is given to our prayer, it would hurt us. There are model prayers we should pray as we fast.

Comparisons of Jabez's Prayer and the Lord's Prayer

I discovered that there are some similarities between the prayer of Jabez and the Lord's Prayer. Below is a comparison between this Old Testament prayer model and the New Testament prayer model:

The Prayer of Jabez	The Lord's Prayer	What do they have in common?
An approved model of how we should pray to God.	An approved model of how we should pray to God.	God would not have put them in the Bible if He hadn't approved of them.
Prayed to the God of Israel.	Prayed to our Father, which is in heaven.	Both prayers were prayed to the same and right God.

The Prayer of Jabez	The Lord's Prayer	What do they have in common?
"Keep me from evil...and that thine hand might be with me."	"And lead us not into temptation, but deliver us from evil."	Both prayers ask to escape temptations.
"Bless me indeed,"	"Give us this day our daily bread."	Both prayers ask for inward and outward blessings.

Spiritual Nuggets for Abundant Living

What golden nuggets are we to learn here? First, we learn that a person's character is revealed in his prayers and his prayer life. In other words, we can learn a lot about a person by just knowing when he prays and what he prays. I do not know if I could trust a man who did not pray. If I found out that someone was not a praying person, I would be skeptical about doing business with him or her. We have had a lot of politicians and presidents say in their campaign that they would put prayer back in the schools, yet they do not even pray themselves. It is hard to trust a man who doesn't pray.

Jabez is only on the scene briefly. He enters with his mother bearing him in sorrow. He prays to the God of Israel, God answers his petitions and nothing else is said about him. I don't know much about Jabez, yet I like the man because he is a praying man. I like him because of what he prayed. I don't know about his parents or where he went to school, but I know that he was a humble man with great faith.

Prayers and the prayer life of a person reveal a lot about a person's character.

Secondly, we learn that Jabez's prayer was not just an inward blessing prayer. I honestly believe that if we do not ask God for outward blessings, then we become suspect hypocrites. We should not think of ourselves as so holy that we cannot ask for outward blessings. God already knows the things we desire; therefore, we should express them in prayer. Jabez's prayer opened the door for us to ask God for outward blessings. I believe if we do not at least from time to time ask God for outward blessings, then we fail to demonstrate and give evidence of our faith.

Summary

Once again as we look at Jabez's prayer, we learn that God does not mind us asking for outward blessings. Why? Because God has the power to bless us without spoiling us. When we bless our children, we run the risk of spoiling them. The reason some of our children are so messed up is because we gave them too much. We gave them everything we never had when we were growing up.

> *A person's character is revealed in his prayers and his prayer life.*

God will withhold a blessing if it is not good for us or if we are not ready for it. He is not going to mess us up. God is in the blessing, not messing business.

I challenge all to choose the prayer of Jabez, the Lord's Prayer and Paul's prayers. I challenge those who have read the "McCalep How to be Blessed Test" to choose a prayer, and for three weeks pray one of those prayers on a regular basis while fasting either from 6:00pm until 6:00am or 6:00am until 6:00pm. Then, prepare to receive a blessing because God will shower anyone who is obedient to this plan with many blessings.

God is only a prayer away. So keep on praying, fasting and praising. Praise is a part of prayer and prayer is a part of praise. We may be just one prayer away from the blessing for which we have been asking the Lord. We should keep praying and praising so we do not forfeit our blessings. We need to pray a righteous prayer in the right name and with the right motives.

Part III: The Prayer of a Black Man Named Jabez Study and Review

1. How do we overcome the expectations of a name or circumstances life has dealt us?

   When we have a relationship with God, we can ask him to bless us despite our names. Our relationship with Him far exceeds our relationship with parents or anyone else. God has the power to change our situations and break generational curses.

2. Why is Jabez's prayer such a powerful prayer?

   Jabez's prayer is a righteous prayer that was prayed to the right God with the right motives. As a result, God answered Jabez's prayer. The prayer of Jabez provides us a biblically approved model for prayer. Another remarkable thing about this prayer is that it has caused people to pray who have never talked to God before.

3. How will your prayers be different as a result of what we learned from Jabez's prayer?

   Consider your prayer life. What lessons from Jabez's prayer can you apply to your personal prayers?

4. Is God calling you to expand your territory and increase your coast? If so, what is He calling you to do? What is preventing you from acting on God's will?

   Spend time in prayer and meditation. Seek God's face. Listen and be honest in your answer. Remember, God already knows the truth.

5. What pain in your past do you need to deal with? How is it affecting your relationships—with God, your family, your Christian brothers and sisters and other people?

If there is pain in your past, deal with it. Unresolved issues do not go away. They only fester. If we are going to be all that God wants us to be, we have to deal with the pain in our past.

6. Look at Jabez's Prayer, the Lord's Prayer and Paul's prayers. Consider praying one of these prayers over the next three weeks while fasting from 6:00 a.m. to 6:00 p.m. or 6:00 p.m. to 6:00 a.m. Keep a prayer journal during the three weeks to record your petitions and God's answers.

This exercise requires discipline. If you will commit to fasting and praying consistently for three weeks, I assure you God will bless your obedience.

Part IV:

A Goodly Heritage

CLAIMING OUR GOODLY HERITAGE

Genesis 25: 29–34

29And Jacob sod pottage: and Esau came from the field, and he was faint: 30And Esau said to Jacob, Feed me, I pray thee, with that same red pottage; for I am faint: therefore was his name called Edom. 31And Jacob said, Sell me this day thy birthright. 32And Esau said, Behold, I am at the point to die: and what profit shall this birthright do to me? 33And Jacob said, Swear to me this day; and he sware unto him: and he sold his birthright unto Jacob. 34Then Jacob gave Esau bread and pottage of lentils; and he did eat and drink, and rose up, and went his way: thus Esau despised his birthright.

Psalm 16:5–6

5The Lord is the portion of mine inheritance and of my cup: thou maintainest my lot. 6The lines are fallen unto me in pleasant places; yea, I have a goodly heritage.

Colossians 3:24–25

24Knowing that of the Lord ye shall receive the reward of the inheritance; for ye serve the Lord Christ. 25But he that doeth wrong shall receive for the wrong which he hath done: and there is no respect of persons.

1 Peter 1:3–4

3Blessed be the God and Father of our Lord Jesus Christ, which according to his abundant mercy hath begotten us again unto a lively hope by the resurrection of Jesus Christ from the dead, 4To an inheritance incorruptible, and undefiled, and that fadeth not away, reserved in heaven for you.

There is an inheritance reserved in heaven for us. The psalmist, David, refers to it as a goodly heritage. David was the one who slew Goliath with a stone. He was a fugitive from King Saul and once from his own son. He was also the murderer of Uriah, and an adulterer with Uriah's wife, Bathsheba; yet, he said that he had a goodly heritage. Whatever our plight may be, no matter how bad, no matter how small, we too have a goodly heritage in the Lord. If we claim God as our Father, we have a goodly heritage.

David inherited land in Bethlehem, but could not claim it as long as King Saul was on the throne. Imagine owning about 100 acres of land in your hometown that is selling for $50,000–$75,000 a lot, but you cannot claim it because the mob or someone evil is after you. That was David's dilemma. As a fugitive, he stood on a mountain claiming to have a goodly heritage. He knew he had a goodly heritage because he knew his inheritance was in the Lord.

A Birthright Sold

Abraham's son, Isaac, had twin boys. Esau, was the oldest, strongest, and most favored by Isaac. He was a hairy, athletic hunter. He was the firstborn so he inherited rights to everything. Jacob was born last, holding on to Esau's heel; therefore, he was known as the "grabber."

One day Esau returned home from hunting, tired, hot and hungry. He was so hungry that he sold his birthright to Jacob for a pot of red pottage, which is what we would call lentil soup, today. If Esau had not sold his birthright to Jacob, there would have been the twelve tribes of Esau. The book of

Revelation tells of the twelve tribes of Israel walking into heaven. If Esau had not sold his birthright, the twelve tribes of Esau would be walking into the heavenly gates.

Red Pottage

I am awfully afraid many of us are like Esau. At some point in our lives, we cashed in something that was very valuable to us on a faint of a moment, not thinking of the value of what we were giving up. We traded our heritage for red pottage.

Today, red pottage comes in many forms. Red pottage can come in the form of acceptability. Some of us have traded in our birthright, our inheritance, to be accepted by others. Red pottage can come in the form of popularity. We relate peer pressure to the youth, but adults are just as guilty of yielding to red pottage peer pressure. Red pottage can come in the form of prosperity. God wants us to prosper, but often when we prosper, we lose sight of our purpose. Some of us are buying red pottage everyday when we ought to be about the business of claiming our birthright.

> *The book of Revelation tells of the twelve tribes of Israel walking into heaven. If Esau had not sold his birthright, the twelve tribes of Esau would be walking into the heavenly gates.*

The rate of suicide among black teens has now caught up with that of white youth. Black people never committed suicide nor gave up on God before. Something has gone awry. Something has changed. We have cashed in our birthright. We have relinquished and redeemed our inheritance. God has

WHEN BLACK MEN STRETCH THEIR HANDS TO GOD

been awfully good to us. We have a goodly heritage. We need to be about the business of seeing God's providential hand on this pilgrim journey.

It was the providential hand of God that led the Hebrew children out of bondage and through the Red Sea to freedom, just as it was the providential hand of God that centuries later led African Americans into freedom. The Red Sea was a roadblock for the Israelites, just as slavery, poverty and oppression were obstacles to African Americans. We praise God for a goodly heritage. Our forefathers put it best when they said, "Masa Lincoln signed the papers, but it was the Lord God that set us free." We have a goodly heritage that should not be given away.

The African-American Believer's First Claim Ticket

Everyone knows that a claim ticket can be turned in to get something. Imagine having three of them. Usually claim tickets have an expiration date, but ours do not. What are we going to do with these claim tickets? We are going to give them to Saint Peter before entering into the heavenly gates because there is an undefiled, incorruptible and non-fading inheritance waiting for us there.

Our first claim ticket says *"We Are a People of the Book."* Southern Baptist Christians hold an annual convention to debate the infallible and inerrant Word of God, who is a conservative and who is a liberal. Once I participated in the discussion and told them that it was a white folk's problem because African Americans never had that problem. I said:

"God has given us the gift of grace to be able to spiritualize what the Bible says is truth. It does not matter whether it is historical material or parables. It does not matter if Jonah was a historical person in the whale or not. He was in the whale, that was the truth, and that is all we need to know."

We need to hold on to our heritage and our Bibles. The Bible was the only textbook our ancestors had. The "masa" taught a few slaves to read the Bible. They had a reason for teaching them. They wanted them to read Ephesians 6:5, which tells the slave to obey his master. But that was the biggest mistake the masa ever made. Reading God's Word and the power of God were the weapons that set the slaves free.

Just as reading set our ancestors free, it can set our young people free today, if they will get their minds off television and onto the Bible. Our young people need to let their fingers do the walking through the pages of truth, *The Holy Bible*. They need to read the book of Exodus where

> *Reading God's Word and the power of God were the weapons that set the slaves free.*

God told Moses to go down and tell old Pharaoh to set His people free. They need to flip over to Paul's writings where he proclaimed neither Greek, Jew, Gentile, circumcised, uncircumcised, bond nor free was the answer, but those who have Christ Jesus, have all that matters. He also proclaimed in 2 Corinthians that God is Spirit and in His Spirit there is liberty. Christ Jesus has set us free. Luke 4:18–19 (NIV) says:

> *"The Spirit of the Lord is on me, because he has anointed me to preach good news to the poor. He has sent me to proclaim freedom for the prisoners and recovery of sight for the blind, to release the oppressed, to proclaim the years of the Lord's favor."*

We need to hold on to our claim tickets.

The African-American Believer's Second Ticket

Our second claim ticket says *"We Need to Hold on to Our Son-Ship."* The Bible tells us that all who have received Him, have been given the privilege to be called sons and daughters, and qualify to say "Abba, Father" (Gal. 4:6). *Abba* is an intimate word meaning "daddy." We need to hold on to the fact that God is our Father and Jesus is our elder brother and friend. Heaven is our home and glory is on our horizon. Yes, we have a heavenly inheritance. We are joint heirs to the throne of God. We have a goodly heritage and need to hold on to it.

The American-American's Believer's Third Claim Ticket

Written on our third claim ticket is *"The Music and Worship of the Black Experience."* God has shown me that there will come a day when people of all colors will worship Him the way our forefathers did. Many of us do not know it, but most of the music we listen to today, including country and western, got its roots from the Negro spirituals. This music of sorrow, hope and praise, is still in our society today bringing out the percussion of the drumbeat of the mother country. Gospel music is simply Negro spirituals with more emphasis on praise than sorrow. We should hold on to our music just as we should hold on to our worship.

Before this world ends, everybody will worship the true and living God. Look at what God is doing around the world. Everyone watches CNN World News. In a minute it shows reports from around the world. One day, as I sat watching CNN, I saw people in Czechoslovakia, Romania, Tiamin Square in China and at the Berlin Wall singing our song, "We Shall Overcome." They did not speak our language, but they were singing our song. We have a goodly heritage so hold on to it.

> *We need to hold on to our Son-Ship. The Bible tells us that all who have received Him, have been given the privilege to be called sons and daughters, and qualify to say "Abba, Father."*

Summary

We need to hold on to our Bibles and our Son-ship. We need to hold on to our music and our worship. We need to hold on to our God and our religion. Our God and our religion are more valuable than any form of red pottage. Do not sell our birthright. We have a goodly heritage. Hold on to it.

A CHANGE IN THE ORDER

Genesis 46:20

And unto Joseph in the land of Egypt were born Manasseh and Ephraim, which Asenath the daughter of Poti-pherah priest of On bare unto him.

Genesis 48:11–22

[11]And Israel said unto Joseph, I had not thought to see thy face: and, lo, God hath showed me also thy seed. [12]And Joseph brought them out from between his knees, and he bowed himself with his face to the earth. [13]And Joseph took them both, Ephraim in his right hand toward Israel's left hand, and Manasseh in his left hand toward Israel's right hand, and brought them near unto him. [14]And Israel stretched out his right hand, and laid it upon Ephraim's head, who was the younger, and his left hand upon Manasseh's head, guiding his hands wittingly; for Manasseh was the firstborn. [15]And he blessed Joseph, and said, God, before whom my fathers Abraham and Isaac did walk, the God which fed me all my life long unto this day, [16]The Angel which redeemed me from all evil, bless the lads; and let my name be named on them, and the name of my fathers Abraham and Isaac; and let them grow into a multitude in the midst of the earth. [17]And when Joseph saw that his father laid his right hand upon the head of Ephraim, it displeased him: and he held up his father's hand, to remove it from Ephraim's head unto Manasseh's head. [18]And Joseph said unto his father, Not so, my father: for this is the firstborn; put thy right hand upon his head. [19]And his father refused, and said, I know it, my son, I know it: he also shall become a people, and he also shall be great: but truly his younger brother shall be greater than he, and his seed shall become a multitude of nations. [20]And he blessed them that day, saying, In thee shall Israel bless, saying, God make thee as Ephraim and as Manasseh: and he set Ephraim before Manasseh. [21]And Israel said unto

Joseph, Behold, I die: but God shall be with you, and bring you again unto the land of your fathers. 22Moreover I have given to thee one portion above thy brethren, which I took out of the hand of the Amorite with my sword and with my bow.

1 Chronicles 5:1–2 (KJV)

1Now the sons of Reuben the firstborn of Israel, (for he was the firstborn; but, forasmuch as he defiled his father's bed, his birthright was given unto the sons of Joseph the son of Israel: and the genealogy is not to be reckoned after the birthright. 2For Judah prevailed above his brethren, and of him came the chief ruler; but the birthright was Joseph's).

First Chronicles 5:1–2 tells us that there was a change in the order of the birthright of Israel's sons. Reuben was the first son of Jacob (Israel), but because he slept with his father's wife, he lost his birthright. Therefore, God reached back and pulled Judah into first place. God reached all the way back beyond Simeon, the second son, and Levi, the third son, and pulled Judah, the tribe of praise to the front of the line. Not only did God reach back and make Judah first, but He also gave Reuben's birthright to Joseph.

When Israel went to war, the tribe of praise went out before the army. Even in the book of Revelation, when the tribes line up in the temple, the tribe of praise is on the east side. Both David, our earthly messiah, and Jesus, our heavenly messiah, came out of the tribe of praise. In the book of Revelation, it is the Lion of

> *God has the power to change the order.*

Judah who breaks the seal in God's heavenly book. So here we learn of the change in order and the preeminent place the tribe of praise has in the kingdom of God.

It is a good thing that God has the power to change the order. There may have been times when we were in last place, but we can now praise God for changing the order. Some of us were told that we would not be successful or would not amount to much, yet we are still holding on. When I was growing up, my head was the subject of my low-esteem. People would plunk my head. They even gave me nicknames like flattop, flat head and wopsy, but now everywhere I go, people compliment my pretty gray hair. My hair has now become the subject of my high-esteem, because God changed the order.

Joseph, the Favorite Son

Joseph was one of Jacob's twelve sons. In fact, he was Jacob's favorite son, and his brothers did not like it. His brothers detested, despised and hated Joseph because of their father's favoritism toward him. His father even gave him a coat of colors, which showed how much he favored him. Eventually, his brothers threw him in a pit and left him there to die, but the Ishmaelites came along and purchased him. The Ishmaelites bought Joseph from his brothers and then sold him into slavery in Africa. The Ishmaelites were descendants of Abraham's oldest son, Ishmael. His mother was Hagar, a black slave girl who was servant to Sarah, Abraham's wife. Ishmael had twelve sons. They were the nomadic tribes of Arabia, which included Midian, and became the Arab nation of today. But God was in the business of changing the order and Joseph quickly became prominent.

Joseph, the Accused Rapist and Prisoner

The Ishmaelites (Midianites) sold Joseph to Potiphar, an Egyptian officer in Pharaoh's court and captain of the guard. Potiphar's wife desired Joseph and tried to seduce him. Joseph turned her down and she cried rape. He went to prison for this false accusation, but God changed the order for him even in prison.

Joseph, the Prime Minister of Egypt

Eventually, Joseph rose to prominence again and became the Prime Minister of Agriculture for Egypt. He was second in command only to Pharaoh. A famine came to the land during the time that he was Prime Minister. Because of Joseph's wise administration, Egypt was the one country with food. Through this turn of events, he ended up feeding his father and brothers.

Sometime after reuniting with his family, Joseph's father died. His brothers feared that he would retaliate against them for their putting him in a pit and selling him into slavery. His brothers thought that as long as their father was alive, Joseph would not bother them, but when he died, they thought perhaps he would want to get even. They approached Joseph

> *Joseph was a Jewish man who had two sons by a gentile, African woman, Asenath, whose father was Poti-pherah, the priest of On.*

with great fear, but he told them *"Ye thought evil against me; but God meant it unto good" (Genesis 50:20)*. Joseph knew that all things work for the good of those who love the Lord and are called according to His purpose.

Joseph, the Father

Joseph was a Jewish man who had two sons by a gentile, African woman, Asenath, whose father was Poti-pherah, the priest of On. On was an ancient city in Egypt known for its school of priests. The priests of On were noted for being the most learned of all the Egyptians. Thus, Asenath, whose name means "wisdom," was the daughter of an African priest who was one of the most learned men in all of Africa.

Joseph's sons were Ephraim and Manasseh. In Genesis 41:51–52, we learn that *Manasseh* means "forget all my toil and all my father's house." *Manasseh* translated in English means "amnesia." *Ephraim* means "fruitful in the land of my affliction." In English, *Ephraim* means "doubly fruitful."

God sometimes speaks to us through our names. God wanted to encourage Manasseh to forget his hard times growing up because He was going to change the order in Manasseh's life. Now that we know our true names—heirs to the throne of God, children of God, brothers and sisters of Jesus Christ—we too can forget the hard times we had growing up in the inner city or working from sun up to sun down in the cotton fields. God has made us fruitful in the land of our oppressors because He is in the business of changing the order.

A Double Portion for the African Boys

Jacob's eyes were dim, for he was about to die. Joseph took his two little African-born boys, who had to be around seventeen at this time, to his father Jacob for a blessing. Jacob lined up Manasseh on his right because he was the older and Ephraim on his left because he was the younger. But when old dimmed-eyed, nearly blind Jacob, got ready to bless the boys, he changed the order and crossed his hands. Immediately, Joseph told him that he didn't know what he was doing and tried to move his father's hands, but Jacob assured Joseph that he did know what he was doing; he was changing the order of things. He told them that both would be blessed, but the younger son would be greater than the older. Jacob said that they were his, just as Reuben and Simeon, and blessed them both with a double portion.

Jacob honored Joseph's sons as if they were his own. Remember, Israel (Jacob) had twelve sons, but only ten of them made up the twelve tribes of Israel. Joseph's sons, Ephraim and Manasseh, were the other two tribes of Israel. Joseph was never part of the twelve tribes because he lived among the Egyptians as Pharaoh's Prime Minister. Therefore, his sons took his place. Levi was not part of the twelve tribes because his family, the Levites, were the priests of the Israelites. The Levites were responsible for ministering and caring for

> *Because Ephraim and Mannaseh represent twenty percent of the twelve tribes of Israel, at least twenty percent of the Jewish nation have black, African ancestors.*

the temple. They were appointed priests because they were the only tribe that stood against the people who worshipped the golden calf. Recently, DNA testing has proven that the Levi tribe were dark-skinned as some have claimed.

Those who condemn any intermingling or intermarriage between races can see that it has existed from the origin of the races. Because Ephraim and Mannaseh represent twenty percent of the twelve tribes of Israel, at least twenty percent of the Jewish nation have black, African ancestors.

A Change in the Order Today

Some twenty-five years ago when Greenforest Community Baptist Church was located on Shamrock Drive in Decatur, Georgia, it was a predominantly white congregation. Then ten families joined who happened to be African Americans. On one Sunday, the preacher and all but three of the white members walked out. We now refer to this as the Greenforest Exodus Experience. The ten African-American families were hurt that their white brothers and sisters literally walked out because they came in, but all things work together for those who love the Lord. Now, Greenforest Community Baptist Church has over 6,000 members. God is still in the business of changing the order.

The Southern Baptist Convention was formed in Augusta, Georgia in 1845 for the explicit purpose of having a religious institution that would condone slavery. In the Georgia Dome, on the 150th anniversary celebration of the Southern Baptist Convention, a white woman who was a delegate from Mississippi encouraged the convention to adopt a resolution to apologize for the wrongfulness done to African Americans by the Southern Baptist Convention. An overwhelming vote was cast to adopt a "Declaration of Repentance," a resolution to ask forgiveness. God is in the business of changing the order.

Our dilemma is trying to change the order by our own strength, but we do not have the power to change the order of God. Instead, we must learn to wait for God.

Summary

Joseph was left in a pit to die, but God changed the order. He was imprisoned, but God changed the order. He was a nobody, but God made him a somebody. He went from zero to hero. He was in a pasture, but God put him in a palace. God changed the order.

We were lost, but now we are found. We were in the world playing on the devil's team, but now we are in the kingdom of God. We were sinners, but now we are saints. Some of us were drunks, but now we are sober. Some of us were once sick, but now we are well. God changed the order. God not only changed the order, He also gave us a double portion.

When Jesus died, the law stepped down and grace stood up. Jesus changed the order when justice stood up and mercy moved to the front of the line. We were found guilty and Jesus freed us with a pardon. We should have died, but Jesus took our place and died for us.

I was told that I was a dumb jock who wouldn't make it. I was called Alabama-bred, one-room schoolhouse educated, segregation socialized, burdened by oppression, black-faced, kinky-haired, thick-lipped, big-nosed and lopside-headed; yet, God changed the order. He gave me a double portion of His love, grace and mercy. Today, I am still all that I was called, but now I know that it only means that I am fearfully and wonderfully made (Psalm 139:14). Yes, God has the power to change the order and if we abide in Him, He will bless us with a double portion.

GOD UNDERSTANDS
EBONICS

Psalm 139:1–16 (NIV)

[1]O Lord, you have searched me and you know me. [2]You know when I sit and when I rise; you perceive my thoughts from afar. [3]You discern my going out and my lying down; you are familiar with all my ways. [4]Before a word is on my tongue you know it completely, O Lord. [5]You hem me in—behind and before; you have laid your hand upon me. [6]Such knowledge is too wonderful for me, too lofty for me to attain. [7]Where can I go from your Spirit? Where can I flee from your presence? [8]If I go up to the heavens, you are there; if I make my bed in the depths, you are there. [9]If I rise on the wings of the dawn, if I settle on the far side of the sea, [10]even there your hand will guide me, your right hand will hold me fast. [11]If I say, "Surely the darkness will hide me and the light become night around me," [12]even the darkness will not be dark to you; the night will shine like the day, for darkness is as light to you. [13]For you created my inmost being; you knit me together in my mother's womb. [14]I praise you because I am fearfully and wonderfully made; your works are wonderful, I know that full well. [15]My frame was not hidden from you when I was made in the secret place. When I was woven together in the depths of the earth, [16]your eyes saw my unformed body. All the days ordained for me were written in your book before one of them came to be.

In recent years, Ebonics has been recognized as a language, a means of communication that is unique and peculiar to black culture. Ebonics, Black English or Ebony-onics has its roots in our African struggle through and out of slavery in America. Some time ago while visiting West Africa, much to my surprise, I learned that there were eleven different languages with even more dialects spoken within the small geographical area from where our ancestors were stolen. Most of our African ancestors were taken from West Africa along the Gambia River and the the Ivory Coast. They were either dropped off in the Caribbean or taken to the shores of Virginia, South Carolina and Georgia where they were eventually sold into slavery. I gained a sense of understanding that I never had before. We can only imagine our forefathers locked up in a dungeon and not being able to communicate with each other. Much of what we call Ebonics has its roots in that history.

> *Most of our African ancestors were taken from West Africa along the Gambia River and the Ivory Coast.*

Ebonics gained national attention several years ago when the Oakland school system proposed to make it a second language. Those who made the proposition explained that other cultures learn standard English best when it is translated from their native language. In other words, Asians learn English best when it is translated from their Asian language, the French learn English best when it is translated from French, and the Spanish learn English best when it is translated from Spanish.

Now a word of clarification, everyone needs to know that in order to live and achieve in white America, we must be able to properly use standard English. This is what the Oakland school system sought to accomplish with their teachers and students. They wanted to train their teachers to recognize "He be standing" to mean "He is standing." They wanted the teachers to be able to recognize "He gone to tha stow" to mean "He went to the store" or that "He was hit by the man and wan't bothin' nobody" to mean "The

> *"God be knowin' yo stuff and it's all good" simply means that God understands us completely and we are fearfully and wonderfully made.*

police beat him up and he wasn't bothering anybody." The Oakland school system shocked the whole academic community when they proposed to teach Ebonics as a stepping-stone to standard English.

I gave this brief scenario to simply tell us that God does not need a translator to hear our cries and prayers. We can talk to God in any way we want, for He hears and pities our every groan. The psalmist tells us that there is not a word from our mouths that God does not understand. God understands Spanish, Japanese, Chinese, Pig Latin and even Ebonics.

God Be Knowin' Yo Stuff and It's All Good

"God be knowin' yo stuff and it's all good" simply means that God understands us completely and we are fearfully and wonderfully made. He knows our every thought, word, deed, emotion, pain, doubt and sin. God is our creator and we are fearfully and wonderfully made. He did not make any mistakes or junk. Everything He made is good.

David explains God's universal understanding in Psalm 139. The Psalm explains how God always understands everything there is to understand about us. He knows the thoughts in our minds even before we think them. He knows every word to be spoken on our lips before it is spoken because it is conceived in our hearts. God hears what is in our hearts. Geography or language is no boundary or barrier for God. He sees, hears, searches and understands all completely. There is not a word He does not understand. Yet, we have a hard time believing that He does. We need to know in our hearts that "God be knowin' yo stuff and it's all good."

> *Most of us suffer from what I call "Spiritual Attention Deficit" (S.A.D.). God cannot get our attention long enough for us to know He knows our pain, so we forfeit His healing power.*

S.A.D.

God has a hard time getting our attention and holding it long enough for us to benefit from His understanding of us. Most of us suffer from what I call "Spiritual Attention Deficit" (S.A.D.). God cannot get our attention long enough for us to know He knows our pain, so we forfeit His healing power. We often forget that God knows our loneliness, so we forfeit His comfort and His love. God cannot get our attention long enough for us to understand that He knows our every sin, so we forfeit His grace and mercy. We forget that God knows our every weakness, so we forfeit His strength. We forget that God hears and knows our every word, so we forfeit the power of prayer. We can talk to God any way we want, even if we say, "I be hurtin'" or "I be in pain" or "I be distressed and suppressed." God understands and He hears our faintest cry.

We forget that God is an all-seeing God, so we forfeit His power of conviction. If we remember that God sees us in the night just like He does in the day, we would not do some of the things we do at night. If we realized that God sees us behind closed doors just like He sees us through open doors, we would not do some of the things we do behind closed doors. The psalmist tells us in verse 12 that God is as light in the night and that night and day are the same as far as His knowing power is concerned. We like to hide in the dark, in a corner, in the back of a room, behind closed doors. God is letting us know today that He sees us in our hiding places.

I am reminded of a man who bragged about how smart his mule was. He often told the story of how he would he say, "Giddy up" to the mule and the mule would respond by going. He would say, "Hold" and the mule would respond by stopping. And so he bragged on his mule to his friends. Then one day, he said, "Giddy up" to the mule, but the mule wouldn't go. Then, he said, "Hold" to the mule, but the mule was already not moving. So he walked around the mule with a 2x4 and hit him in the head right between the eyes. Afterwards, he said, "Giddy-up" to the mule and the mule started to move. He said, "Hold" to the mule and the mule stopped. My point is that God should not have to hit us in the head with a 2x4 to get our attention. He sees, knows, hears and understands all.

Whether we take the wings of the morning and fly to the utmost parts of the earth, He is there. If we make our bed in hell, He is there. God is everywhere and He is trying to get our attention.

We Can Run, But We Can't Hide

God is telling us that we can run, but we can't hide. Jonah tried to run, but he couldn't hide. God told Jonah to go to Nineveh, but he caught a ship going in the other direction to Tarshish instead. God caught up with Jonah and turned him around by putting him in the belly of a whale for three days and three nights, and then spitting him out on dry land. Jonah had to learn that he could run, but he could not hide from God. Sometimes people do not want to commit to God because they do not want to give up their sinful pleasures, so they run and hide from Him. However, the truth is, we can run, but we can't hide.

I ran from God for nearly twenty years. I told Him over and over again that I was not worthy. I tried to hide in sin, ambition, work, achievement and success. I even tried to hide in alcohol. I tried to run, but I couldn't hide. God kept telling me that He knew everything I had ever done. He told me that I was His choice because I was fearfully and wonderfully made. I ran, but I couldn't hide.

God wants to get our attention. Don't let Him have to get it with a 2x4. When God tugs, surrender.

Fearfully and Wonderfully Made

God created us and we are fearfully and wonderfully made. I find the word *fearfully* to be a very interesting description of a human being. How are we fearfully made? Someone once told me that if a man could stand on the outside and look at the work God is doing for him on the inside, he would shake and tremble with fear. Just think of our physiological systems and how God has worked it all out. He uniquely put our circulatory, respiratory, digestive, endocrine and nervous systems together to work in perfect unison, and that makes us fearfully and wonderfully made.

Consider what God does with the digestion of a sandwich. At the moment we put a hamburger in our mouths, God starts working on it for our good. He takes the bread and churns it. He takes the meat and churns it. He takes the mayo, mustard and anything else we might have put on our hamburger, and He uses all of it to give us energy in our blood

> *God created us and we are fearfully and wonderfully made.*

cells. God wants us to know that we are fearfully and wonderfully made. When we truly know it, we will not be depressed or suicidal.

We are somebody through Christ Jesus. Black children in America need to know that their sugar is as sweet as anybody else's, just as our minds are as keen as anybody else's and our hair is as good as anybody else's. Older blacks need to cast out the spirit that straight hair is good. What makes straight hair good and kinky hair (curly hair) bad? We need to understand that kinky hair is just as good as any other kind of hair. To say that straight hair is good hair implies that non-straight hair must be bad hair. This is a subtle form of self-hatred and devaluing of oneself.

This psychology enters the minds of young black children and destroys their self-worth. When a young black child takes a gun and points it at another black child, he is telling that other child that he is blowing him away because he is of no value. We have already told him that he is inferior and it has been locked into his brain. If he pulls the trigger, we gave him a psychological excuse to blow somebody's brains out or his own.

My kinky hair as well as my black skin is also fearfully and wonderfully made. My broad nose and big lips are fearfully and wonderfully made. Sisters, your big hips are fearfully and wonderfully made. I praise God because I am fearfully and wonderfully made. I thank Him for my coarse hair, black skin, big nose and big lips. I also thank Him for the sisters with big hips. Yes, I am fearfully and wonderfully made!

God Understands All Languages

We can talk to God in any language we want and He will understand. God will hear our cries and prayers. A songwriter once wrote, "I love the Lord and He heard my cry and He pitied my every groan. Long as I live and trouble rise I will hasten to his throne." I am not worried about Ebonics. I will let the educators solve that problem. I want us to know that God understands Ebonics and any other kind of bonics because He is an all-understanding God. He demonstrated His understanding on the cross when he cried, "Eli, Eli, lama sabachthani?" (Matt. 27:46). They thought He was speaking to Elijah, but He was talking to God. He was not speaking in the language of the New Testament. He was not speaking in Hebrew or Greek. He was talking in a strange Aramaic language with a Samaritan dialect. He said, "Eli, Eli—My God, My God, why has thou forsaken me?" It does not matter what language we use, God will understand.

Summary

"God be knowin' yo stuff and it's all good." God knows everything about us. He understands us totally and completely because He knows our heart. We are fearfully and wonderfully made. We can run, but we can't hide from God no matter how much Spiritual Attention Deficit we have. It is time to stop running *from* God and start running *to* Him. God understands us no matter what language we use, for He is the one who has knitted us together. Yes, we are fearfully and wonderfully made!

THE VOICE OF THE BLOOD OF THE SLAUGHTERED

Genesis 4:9–10 (NKJV)

9Then the Lord said to Cain, "Where is Abel your brother?" He said, "I do not know. Am I my brother's keeper?" 10And He said, "What have you done? The voice of your brother's blood cries out to Me from the ground."

Mark 14:22–26 (NKJV)

22 And as they were eating, Jesus took bread, blessed and broke it, and gave it to them and said, "Take, eat; this is My body." 23Then He took the cup, and when He had given thanks He gave it to them, and they all drank from it. 24And He said to them, "This is My blood of the new covenant, which is shed for many. 25Assuredly, I say to you, I will no longer drink of the fruit of the vine until that day when I drink it new in the kingdom of God." 26And when they had sung a hymn, they went out to the Mount of Olives.

Revelation 6:9–11 (NKJV)

9 When He opened the fifth seal, I saw under the altar the souls of those who had been slain for the word of God and for the testimony which they held. 10And they cried with a loud voice, saying, "How long, O Lord, holy and true, until You judge and avenge our blood on those who dwell on the earth?" 11Then a white robe was given to each of them; and it was said to them that they should rest a little while longer, until both the number of their fellow servants and their brethren, who would be killed as they were, was completed.

The freedom African Americans are experiencing today was paid for by the blood of our slaughtered ancestors. Just as the freedom from the penalty of sin we are experiencing today was paid for by the blood of our slaughtered Savior, Jesus Christ. When I was in elementary school, everyday before class started, we gathered for devotion and sang the Negro National Anthem, "Lift Every Voice and Sing" by James Weldon Johnson. Little black boys and girls in the deep south of Alabama gathered in a one-room schoolhouse singing a song that helped to build their self-esteem. The words to this song instilled pride in whose we were, who we were, where we had come from and where we were going. The words of this song echoed through our very souls. James Weldon Johnson captured in this song the fact that those of us living today are now benefiting from the great sacrifices of those who have gone before us—Nat Turner, Martin Luther King Jr., Malcolm X, Emmett Till, Medgar Evers, Bobby Kennedy, President John F. Kennedy and many others. They all died for the cause of justice and freedom. The voice of the blood of the slaughtered cries out to us for a response. Sacrificed blood demands and expects a response.

Listen to the Voice of the Blood

In the book of Genesis, two brothers, Cain and Abel, made sacrificial offerings to God. Abel's offering was accepted, but Cain's was not. Cain became jealous of Abel and killed him out of vengeance. God asked Cain about what he had done and Cain replied, "Am I my brother's keeper?" God responded by telling Cain that Abel's blood cried out from the ground for

Him. Abel's blood was crying out for God to deal with the injustice he had suffered.

The voice of the blood of the slaughtered is crying out for a better sacrifice. Abel gave a better sacrifice and Cain slew him. God is calling us to make a better sacrifice than what we are doing right now. Wherever we are in our Christian life, God wants us to know today that a better sacrifice is required of us. Jesus gave a better sacrifice. He shed sacrificial blood so that we might have a right to the tree of

> *Sacrificed blood demands and expects a response.*

life. The voice of the blood-stained Savior is calling to us saying, "I want a better sacrifice from you. Present your body as a living sacrifice, holy and acceptable unto Me, which is your reasonable service."

No Appreciation for Past Sacrifices

Our problem today is that we do not appreciate those who have sacrificed for us in the past. The blood of the slaughtered was spilled for us to have the right to vote; yet we lay in bed and refuse to vote on election day, especially if it is raining. The blood of the slaughtered fought for the right to integrate schools; yet, many of our children do not care about going to school today. Sadly, many African-American teachers and parents do not care about teaching our children.

There is no appreciation for those who sacrificed their lives for us, just as there is no appreciation for the sacrificially shed blood of Jesus Christ. We honor the fact that He died for the pardon of our sins, but we cheapen what He did. We become saved, but continue to participate in sinful acts, such as adultery, fornication, stealing, fighting and killing each other. God gave His only Son so that we might have the right to abundant life now and eternal life forever. Why do we cheapen His grace? We do not even take His Holy Communion seriously. As they drank of the cup, Jesus told the disciples they were drinking His blood that would be shed for a sacrifice. The bread was His body that would be broken for our sins. The spilled, sacrificial blood of Jesus demands a response from us.

> *The spilled, sacrificial blood of Jesus demands a response from us.*

God Will Avenge the Blood of the Righteous

God will avenge the blood of the righteous. In the book of Revelation, John looked into the future and envisioned saints who died for the cause of Christ waiting in glory asking, "God, how long will you wait to avenge the blood of those who were slaughtered for the sake of righteousness?" It is not a question of will God avenge them, but a matter of when. Someday the wicked will cease from troubling and the weary will be at rest. Someday God will avenge the blood of the righteous.

Learning to Respect Ourselves

An appreciation for those who came before us will help us respect ourselves. Those of us who are doing well today are standing on the wings of the blood of the slaughtered. Every black major league baseball player is standing on the blood-stained wing of Jackie Robinson. The phenomenal tennis playing Williams sisters are standing on the blood-stained wings of Althea Gibson. Tiger Woods is standing on the blood-stained wings of Lee Elder. Every black lawyer and judge is standing on the blood-stained wings of Thurgood Marshall. Every black educator is standing on the wings of Mary McLeod Bethune. The list could go on and on. If we do not appreciate who we are and where we are, we will never realize that we are standing on the blood-stained wings of the slaughtered that came before us.

Summary

The voice of the blood of the slain Lamb is calling us to put our all on the altar. Jesus is calling someone to salvation and someone else to rededication. Jesus is calling someone to commit to Him and to make Him Lord of his or her life. Jesus is calling all of us to present our bodies as living sacrifices, holy and acceptable to

> *An appreciation for those who came before us will help us respect ourselves.*

Him, which is our reasonable service. The voice of the blood of the slaughtered is calling us and it demands a response.

Part IV: A Goodly Heritage
Study and Review

1. In what ways has God demonstrated His power to change the order of things in your life?

   Think about times when God made the impossible possible in your life. How has God demonstrated His grace and mercy to you?

2. Why is it important for our children to know that God is in the business of changing the order?

   Our children need to know no matter how bleak a situation may appear, God has the power to change things. No matter how they have sinned, Jesus has the power to forgive them and to make them new creatures. If our children will abide in God, He will bless them with a double portion.

3. What things do we need to hold on to when claiming our heritage as African-American Christians? Why?

   As African-American Christians, we need to hold on to the goodly heritage God has given us. We need to hold on to our God and our religion. We need to hold on to our Son-ship and we need to hold on to our music and worship experience. We were included in God's redemptive plan from the beginning. We are not an afterthought. We are His children. We are people of the Bible and we have a goodly heritage.

4. Why is it important for us to know that God understands Ebonics?

We need to know that God understands any language. We can cry out to Him in standard English, Latin or Ebonics. He loves us. He will hear us and He will answer.

5. What does it mean to you personally to be *fearfully and wonderfully made*?

Look in the mirror. God made you. He knitted you together in your mother's womb and said you were good. Do you truly know how wonderful you are?

6. In what ways have you been hiding from God?

I encourage you to pray, fast and seek God's face. Then, be honest with yourself and God in answering this question. Do not be afraid to face God. We can run, but we cannot hide. He knows where we are and what we are doing. If you have been running or hiding from God, it is time to surrender.

7. What would you do differently if you were constantly aware of God watching you at all times?

This is another opportunity to face God and own up to the things that we are doing that may not be pleasing in His sight. Confess, repent and turn away from anything that is separating you from God.

8. "God be knowin' yo stuff and it's all good." How does it make you feel to know that God knows everything about you?

   At times, the thought that God knows everything is frightening. However, there are times when that thought brings comfort and assurance. Which is true for you?

9. Whose blood-stained wings are you standing on? What can you do to have a greater appreciation of the sacrifice others made for you?

   Consider where you are in life. Whose sacrifice made it possible for you to be where you are? How much do you appreciate what others have done for you?

10. Jesus is calling for a better sacrifice from all Christians. How will you respond?

    Jesus is calling all Christians to present themselves as living sacrifices. His voice demands a response. What is yours?

Part V:

Samaritans in the Bible

A GOOD BLACK SAMARITAN
God Used a Person of Color to Teach the World What Is Good

John 4:1–4 (NIV)

¹The Pharisees heard that Jesus was gaining and baptizing more disciples than John, ²although in fact it was not Jesus who baptized, but his disciples. ³When the Lord learned of this, he left Judea and went back once more to Galilee. ⁴Now he had to go through Samaria.

John 4:9 (NIV)

The Samaritan woman said to him, "You are a Jew and I am a Samaritan woman. How can you ask me for a drink?" (For Jews do not associate with Samaritans.)

John 4:28–30 (NIV)

²⁸Then, leaving her water jar, the woman went back to the town and said to the people, ²⁹"Come, see a man who told me everything I ever did. Could this be the Christ?" ³⁰They came out of the town and made their way toward him.

John 4:39–41 (NIV)

³⁹Many of the Samaritans from that town believed in him because of the woman's testimony, "He told me everything I ever did." ⁴⁰So when the Samaritans came to him, they urged him to stay with them, and he stayed two days. ⁴¹And because of his words many more became believers.

Luke 10:33 (KJV)

But a certain Samaritan, as he journeyed, came where he was: and when he saw him, he had compassion on him.

Luke 17:12–16 (KJV)

[12]And as he entered into a certain village, there met him ten men that were lepers, which stood afar off: [13]And they lifted up their voices, and said, Jesus, Master, have mercy on us. [14]And when he saw them, he said unto them, Go show yourselves unto the priests. And it came to pass, that, as they went, they were cleansed. [15]And one of them, when he saw that he was healed, turned back, and with a loud voice glorified God, [16]And fell down on his face at his feet, giving him thanks: and he was a Samaritan.

Acts 8:3–6 (KJV)

[3]As for Saul, he made havock of the church, entering into every house, and haling men and women committed them to prison. [4]Therefore they that were scattered abroad went every where preaching the word. [5]Then Philip went down to the city of Samaria, and preached Christ unto them. [6]And the people with one accord gave heed unto those things which Philip spake, hearing and seeing the miracles which he did.

Acts 8:14–17 (KJV)

[14]Now when the apostles which were at Jerusalem heard that Samaria had received the word of God, they sent unto them Peter and John: [15]Who, when they were come down, prayed for them, that they might receive the Holy Ghost: [16](For as yet he was fallen upon none of them: only they were baptized in the name of the Lord Jesus.) [17]Then laid they their hands on them, and they received the Holy Ghost.

Once again let me say that in Christ there is no black or white. God is no respecter of persons—Jews or Gentiles. There are no African Americans in the Bible. The Bible does not deal with color. Likewise, there were basically no European Jews in the Old or New Testament. The Jews did not go back to Israel until 1947. The Jews of the Bible were Palestinian Jews. Biblical Jews were not European and the people of color that included the Palestinian Jews, were not African American. However, the Samaritans were people of much color. The point of all this is to simply say that Jesus used people of color to teach the world what is good.

The Answer to Racial Indoctrination of American Symbolism

At an ushers retreat recently, one of the ushers recited the poem entitled *What Shall I Tell My Black Child Who Lives in America?* (See Appendix.) The poem challenges African Americans to think about what to tell their children about being black when every image symbolizing black is bad or evil and that which is good and pure is white. What shall we tell our black child when even dark cake

> *Jesus used people of color to teach the world what is good.*

is devil's food and white cake is angel's food? The poem goes on to contrast imagery in America. What shall we tell our black children?

Well, I have an answer. Tell them that Jesus used people of color to teach the whole world what is good. Opposite from the indoctrination of Western civilization, Jesus used a people of color to teach the whole world what is good. It is difficult to even think or say bad Samaritan. It is an oxymoron. The word Samaritan is always associated with good. There are legal laws on the books that speak of "Good Samaritan." Jesus used a people of color to illustrate to the entire world what is good.

The Origin of Samaria

When God's people, the Israelites, misbehaved over and over again after warnings from all of the prophets, the nation of Assyria, brought them into captivity. Then the king of Assyria, for whatever reason, imported men from Babylon. One of them, Hamor, was a direct descendant of Ham. The following Scriptures further explain the origin of the Samaritan people:

2 Kings 17:6–7 (NIV)

6In the ninth year of Hoshea, the king of Assyria captured Samaria and deported the Israelites to Assyria. He settled them in Halah, in Gozan on the Habor River and in the towns of the Medes.

2 Kings 17:22–24 (NIV)

22The Israelites persisted in all the sins of Jeroboam and did not turn away from them 23 until the Lord removed them from his presence, as he had warned through all his servants the prophets. So the people of Israel were taken from their homeland into exile in Assyria, and they are still there. 24The king of Assyria brought people from Babylon, Cuthah, Avva, Hamath and Sepharvaim and settled them in the towns of Samaria to replace the Israelites. They took over Samaria and lived in its towns.

Jesus was born at a time when the Samaritans were discriminated against. Once again, the Bible does not mention color. It is very significant that the whole matter of color and discrimination did not begin until much later. In Bible times, people discriminated against tribes and nations, and God only discriminated against heathens.

Heathens are defined as those who do not know the Lord. God said over and over again not to marry anybody who does not know the Lord. He did not say, "Do not marry anybody of color." In other words, He did not say, "Do not marry anybody who is white." Second Corinthians 6:14 says:

> "Be ye not unequally yoked together with unbelievers: for what fellowship hath righteousness with unrighteousness? and what communion hath light with darkness?"

God said that Christians are not to be unequally yoked. Do not marry anybody who is not equally yoked with you as a Christian.

In John 8:48, when the Pharisees were trying to defame and belittle Jesus, they asked Him if He was a Samaritan with a devil in Him. John 8:48 (KJV) says, "Then answered the Jews, and said unto him, Say we not well that thou art a Samaritan, and hast a devil?" The Pharisees pointed their fingers at Jesus and asked, "Are you a Samaritan with a devil?" Jesus denied that He had a devil in Him, but He did not say that He was not a Samaritan. All He said was, "I don't have a devil in Me. I'm Just about My Father's business." Interestingly, that was all He

> The Pharisees pointed their fingers at Jesus and asked, "Are you a Samaritan with a devil?" Jesus denied that He had a devil in Him, but He did not say that He was not a Samaritan.

said. Maybe He said only that because He, being fully God and fully man, was totally aware that He had Hamitic blood.

Do you want to be a good Samaritan based upon these people of color in the Bible called Samaritans? These are the people of whom Jesus spoke of when He said, *"And he must needs go through Samaria" (John 4:4 NKJV).* Judea was on one side, Galilee was on the other, and Samaria right in the middle. Most Jews would go around Samaria. Even when we visited the Holy Land several years ago, we did not travel through Samaria, we went around it. Jesus said, "I've got to go through the 'hood or inner city. I'm not going around through the suburbs." If you want to be a good Samaritan, then you should explore four points relative to the characteristics of a good Samaritan.

A Good Samaritan is a Witness

First, if you are to be a good Samaritan, you must be a witness. You cannot be a good Samaritan without being a witness. In John 4, Jesus met a Samaritan woman at the well and told her all about herself. When this woman of color came to herself, after Jesus had confronted her with her sins, she dropped her water pot, ran back to the city and told the brothers and girl-friends to come see a man who must be the Christ. She said that this man had told her everything she ever did, so He must be the Christ. The Bible says that because of this woman's testimony many came to know Christ. So if you are going to be a good Samaritan, you must be a witness.

A Good Samaritan Cares for All People

Secondly, if you are going to be a good Samaritan, you must have compassion and care for all people. Herein lies the parable of the good Samaritan in Luke 10. You know the story of how a man came down from Jerusalem to Jericho, fell on bad times and was robbed. He was lying in the street, perhaps close to death. A Levite and a priest came by. Today, we would say a pastor and a deacon came by. The pastor stepped over him and kept going. The deacon crossed to the other side of the road to avoid him and kept going. But a Samaritan, a descendent of Ham, came by and ministered to him. He picked him up, took him to the Marriott Marquis, put an American Express card on him and told them to take care of him. He even went so far as to promise to pay anything else the man owed when he returned.

If you are going to be a good Samaritan you must have compassion and care for all people. Now, *all* means "all." I looked up the word *all* in several languages, and *all* means "all" in every language. It does not matter if a person is white or black. We must have compassion for white people. If a white person is lost and going to hell, we have to have compassion on that person. We cannot be like Jonah. Jonah did not want the people of Nineveh to get saved. He didn't want those heathens to be saved. Some African Americans act like white people deserve to go to hell, but the Word of God says that if any man is in Christ, he is a new creature, the old has passed away and all is become new. So we must have compassion on Africans, Caucasians, Asians, Latinos and all people. If you are going to be a good Samaritan you have to be a witness and have compassion on all people.

A Good Samaritan Is Thankful

To be a good Samaritan, you must be thankful. Jesus used people of color throughout the New Testament to demonstrate what is good. There were ten men in Luke 17:12–19 who were stricken with leprosy. They met Jesus and He healed all ten. The Bible says that only one turned back to say "Thank you." He was a Samaritan. Jesus asked, "Were there not ten? Where are the other nine?"

You do not want to be in the other nine. If you are a good Samaritan, you have to look back and say thank you. God has delivered us out of a lot of leprosy. He delivered African Americans out of the leprosy of slavery, second-class citizenship and Jim Crow laws. He delivered us from the leprosy of poverty. Most importantly, He delivered all Christians from the leprosy of sin. We were all sinners doomed to hell, but God in His compassion delivered us from that leprosy. To be a good Samaritan, you must look back and say, "Thank you."

> *A good Samaritan is available to the Holy Spirit.*

A Good Samaritan Is Available to the Holy Spirit

Finally, if you are going to be a good Samaritan, you must be available to the work of the Holy Spirit. The Bible declares in Acts 8:5 that Philip went down to the city of Samaria and preached Christ to them. Acts 8:14–15 says:

"Now when the apostles which were at Jerusalem heard that Samaria had received the word of God, they sent unto them Peter and John: Who, when they were come down, prayed for them, that they might receive the Holy Ghost."

The point is that the Samaritans in Acts 8 made themselves available to the work and power of the Holy Spirit. If we are going to be good Samaritans, we must do likewise.

Summary

In Christ there is no Jew or Gentile, male or female, black or white. However, America is inundated with symbolism that suggests that black is bad and white is good. Jesus discredited this western thought by using the Samaritans, a people of color, to teach the world, especially the Christian Bible-reading community, that black is good. All Christians (black and white) should want to be good Samaritans. To be a good Samaritan, one must:

- Be a witness to all people.
- Show compassion and care for all people.
- Always look back and be thankful.
- Be available to the work and power of the Holy Spirit.

Part V: Samaritans in the Bible
Study and Review

1. Why did the Samaritans play such a significant role in the Bible?

   Jesus used Samaritans, people of color, throughout the Bible to teach the world what is good.

2. What are the characteristics of a good Samaritan?

   Good Samaritans:
   - Witness to others about Christ.
   - Have compassion for all people, regardless of their race or color.
   - Are thankful for what God has done for them.
   - Are available to the work and power of the Holy Spirit.

3. Why could the woman at the well possibly be the first female evangelist?

   She told everyone what Jesus had done for her. She could not keep it to herself. This woman spread the gospel (good news) and, as a result, many were saved.

4. What is the significance of the one leper returning to thank Jesus for healing him?

   Jesus healed ten lepers. Only one, the Samaritan returned to say, "Thank you." Through this man's example, Jesus teaches us the importance of looking back and saying, "Thank you."

5. What are you doing in your life that you need the work and the power of the Holy Spirit to accomplish?

Often, we do things using our own strength and intelligence; however, the things that God calls us to do are usually beyond our human ability. Someone said, "God does not call the equipped. He equips the called." What has God called you to do that you can only do through Him?

6. A good Samaritan has compassion for all people. Is there any one in your life to whom you should extend more compassion? Are you concerned about the salvation of people of all races?

God has commanded us to be witnesses to the uttermost parts of the world. He instructs us to witness to all people. We cannot reserve salvation for those who look like us. The gospel is for everyone and, as Christians, we are to share it with people of every race.

7. What specifically do you need to do to become a good Samaritan?

Look at your daily life. Are you a good witness? Do you care that all people, regardless of race, are saved? Do you stop and thank God for what He does for you? Are you available to the work and power of the Holy Spirit?

Part VI

The Cushite Movement

THE CUSHITE MOVEMENT

The Cushite Movement is a non-profit, nondenominational Christian men's ministry whose mission is to encourage men to be committed, sincere participants in fulfilling the prophecy that states: When black men stretch their hands to God in submission and adoration, God will bring an unparalleled revival to all His people.

This is accomplished through seminars, conferences, revivals and informational communication that focus on revealing and affirming:

- Our biblical black heritage.
- Specific issues that are relevant to black men.
- The core values and covenant vows of the ministry.

How to Get Involved

The Cushite Movement is not a membership-based organization, rather it is a participatory organization. Those who commit and participate will be recorded as simply "being in the number." Participants are counted in the number if they complete a card committing to the core values of the Cushite Movement while attending a Cushite conference or online at www.thecushitemovement.org.

We encourage you to partner with us in sponsoring a Cushite conference in your local city. For more information, call 404-486-5725.

Scripture Reference

Psalm 68:31 (KJV): *"Princes shall come out of Egypt; Ethiopia shall soon stretch out her hands to God."*

Our Rally Cry

Brother Man, are you in the number?

Our Name

In the Bible, Cush is listed first among the sons of Ham, who is the biblical father of the Negro race. God used Ham and his descendants to play a major role in unfolding His redemptive plan. The Cushite Movement affirms this major role by revealing the biblical black heritage that has been hidden, ignored, denied, misinterpreted and misconstrued.

Our Vision

Our vision is to lead an unparalleled revival of all God's people throughout the land that will result in freedom and victory through revealed truth, submission to the Lordship of Jesus and authentic, expressive praise.

Our Motto

Unashamedly black, unapologetically Christian and vowed to be Christ-like.

Our Origin

The Cushite Movement had its beginning with a God-given prophecy. With the dawn of the new millennium and Y2K chaos of the year 2000, God gave a word of prophecy to Pastor George O. McCalep, Jr. in Decatur, Georgia. With fear and trembling and under the anointing of the Holy Spirit, Pastor McCalep began to communicate the prophecy first to the congregation of Greenforest Community Baptist Church where he serves, then from pulpits across the land, and now every time the opportunity is given. The reception of the prophecy was no less than awesome.

God provided inspiration and affirmation for the movement in several ways from several sources. The following is a reconstructed list of times, places, events, organizations and people God used to bring it all together.

- The Brotherhood (male choir) often referred to as the Cushite Choir at the Greenforest Community Baptist Church, was and is a major source of inspiration and affirmation. They have mirrored the prophecy through their music and worship. Moreover, they have become an active fellowship, supporting one another. Additionally, they are a self-appointed ministry to, as they say, "watch the pastor's back." Their Brotherhood Choir Retreat, coordinated by the enthusiastic Brother Therone Pratter in 2002, at which Pastor McCalep was asked to speak, provided a spark for the Cushite Movement that has proven to be like the inconsumable burning bush.

- The weekly men's discipleship class at Greenforest Community Baptist Church, led by Deacons Melvin McCowan and Charles Buffington, and the monthly men's discipleship training taught by Pastor McCalep, have moved men to be committed followers of Christ, especially in the areas of family, work and church.

- Deacon Eugene Wright's enthusiasm for the annual men's day at Greenforest Community Baptist Church and the willingness of the Brotherhood Ministry, led by Deacon Glenn Dixie, to do anything asked of them (such as cook for the entire church) served as a source of inspiration throughout the entire embryonic period of the movement.

- The passion for black men demonstrated by Attorney Xavier Dicks, Fulfillment Hour (Sunday School) teacher and author of *How to Survive as a Black Man*, has served as an additional catalyst for the movement. Brother Dicks individually promoted, sponsored and hosted a Black Men's Conference at the Georgia World Congress Center in April 2003. The founder of the Cushite Movement, Pastor George O. McCalep, Jr., served as a keynote speaker.

- The many gifted authors, too numerous to name, who have dedicated their lives to the passionate, scholarly pursuit of unveiling the truth about our biblical black heritage and the black presence in the Bible, provide impetus and continuous fuel for the movement.

- The overwhelmingly positive reception and feedback to the sermon series, "Christ-Centered Lessons from

Biblical Black Characters" preached by Pastor McCalep at the Greenforest Community Baptist Church affirmed that there was a real need for the Cushite movement. Support for this series was consistently demonstrated by the sale of the sermon cassette tapes immediately after church. Feedback from members as well as the television viewing audience further confirmed this need. The messages are individually packaged on CDs and are published within this book.

- During a Men's Conference held at the Ridgecrest Conference Center in North Carolina in April 2003, the Brotherhood Choir from Greenforest Community led the praise and worship devotional period. Pastor McCalep simply stated the prophecy while extending the welcome. Afterwards, the conference workshops went on as scheduled. Nothing else was said concerning the prophecy, except two or three men simply said they received it. Noteworthy, the preacher who was to preach the closing sermon was unaware of the prophecy because he was not in attendance during the welcome. However, when the closing preacher finished his sermon and offered an invitation to come to the altar, the Holy Spirit moved nearly two hundred men to almost simultaneously stand and stretch their hands high above their heads in a demonstrative sign of surrender and adoration to God. It was at this point Deacon Melvin McCowan, who is one the major sources of inspiration for the Cushite Movement, and Pastor

McCalep knew for sure that God wanted more than just a loose knit group of men praising Him in isolation.

- On June 7, 2003, the day before Pentecost Sunday, the first annual Cushite Men's Conference was held at the Greenforest McCalep Christian Early Learning Center. The keynote speaker was Rev. William Dwight McKissic, Sr., a noted, gifted and scholarly authority on the subject of the black presence in the Bible and author of *Beyond Roots Volumes One and Two*. The planning committee for the conference consisted of Deacons Charles Buffington, Melvin McCowan, Eugene Wright, Glenn Dixie, and Brothers Tyrone Pratter, Xavier Dicks and Pastor McCalep. All of the planning committee members were asked to serve as the first board of directors for Cushite Movement, Incorporated.

Cushite Core Values

1. We believe that Jesus is God and Lord of our lives. We believe in the pre-existence of Jesus and His second coming. We believe that based on Scriptural genealogy, when Jesus came in the flesh (the incarnated historical Jesus of Nazareth), He chose to come as a man of color who was a Semitic person with African ancestry.

2. We believe that the preached word is the best communication vehicle for unveiling the rich biblical black heritage.

3. We believe that the root of racism is grounded in the failure of the universal Christian church to recognize,

reveal and the truth relative to the Negro, African and black heritage in the Bible.

4. We believe that life, humanity, womanhood, family and marriage should be valued, cherished, respected and protected.

5. We believe that the total presence of a father in the home makes a major difference in the life of children.

6. We believe that a godly family is a mirrored reflection of the church. Therefore, as the head of the family, we should love our wives as Christ loved the church and make every effort to lead our families in all spiritual matters, such as going to church, Bible study, praying and praising.

7. We believe that the church is the body of Christ, Christ is the head of the body, and the pastor, as the under shepherd, represents Christ. Therefore, we believe that the pastor should be followed, respected, protected, loved and lifted up.

8. We believe that through the witnessing of surrender and praise that is seen in our lives, God will bring about an unparalleled spiritual revival to all His people.

9. We believe that our submission to the Lordship of Jesus must include the surrender of our time, money, talents and spiritual gifts to the church in obedience to the Word of God.

10. We believe that every man deserves to hear an authentic witness from a Cushite brother relative to what the Lord has done for him.

Cushite Covenant Vows

1. A Cushite man vows to demonstrate his love for Christ through his living, giving and praise.
2. A Cushite man vows to uphold and share the Cushite Movement's prophecy, vision and core values with as many other men as possible.
3. A Cushite man vows to witness to as well as invite and bring as many other men to as many Cushite conferences and seminars as possible.
4. A Cushite man vows to uphold racial equality and to respect all mankind.
5. A Cushite man vows to sexual purity, fidelity and the sanctity of marriage.
6. A Cushite man vows to bond with other Cushite men, to form prayer partners and accountability partners for encouragement and to help each other uphold the Cushite vows.
7. A Cushite man vows to support the vision and mission of his church, and to love, respect and pray for his pastor.

The Cushite Creed

The Cushite Creed was adapted from the African-American Church Creedal Statement compiled by Dr. Roscoe Cooper, founder and pastor.

Leader: Who are we? Who is the Lord, our God?

People: We are Cushite Christians who are men. Our ancestors were Africans whose families were taken out of their land, but we became a populous people. The people of this land treated us harshly and forced us to work as slaves. Then, we cried out for help to the God of Abraham and Sarah, Isaac and Rebecca, Jacob, Leah and Rachel, and the Father of Jesus Christ.

Leader: What has the Lord, our God done for us?

People: God heard us and saw our suffering, hardship and misery. By God's great power and strength, He saved us from sin to righteousness, from death to life, from slavery to freedom and from oppression to liberation. God worked miracles and wonders and caused terrifying things to happen. God is forever opening doors for us that were once closed.

Leader: What is our response?

People: So we gather on this day as Cushite Christians to offer praise and thanksgiving to God for all that He has done and is doing for us and through us. We offer ourselves and our resources to God that He may, through the presence and power of the Holy Spirit, empower us to live our lives in accordance with His will and to participate in history as agents of God's liberation of the poor and oppressed.

Leader: What about those of other races, nationalities and color who come within our gates?

People: We embrace them as brothers and sisters in the Lord Jesus, as the creation of God and joint heirs with Christ. Their presence here demonstrates their commitment to our cause and we welcome them as siblings, friends and allies.

Appendix

What Shall I Tell My Children Who Are Black?

by

Margaret Taylor Goss Burroughs

(Printed by permission of the author.)

What shall I tell my children who are black
Of what it means to be a captive in this dark skin?
What shall I tell my dear one, fruit of my womb?
O how beautiful they are when everywhere they turn
They are faced with abhorrence of everything that is black.
The night is black and so is the bogeyman.
Villains are black with black hearts.
A black cow gives no milk. A black hen lays no eggs.
Bad news comes bordered in black,
Mourning clothes in black.
Storm clouds, black, black is evil
And evil is black and devils food is black.

What shall I tell my dear ones raised in a white world
A place where white has been made to represent
All that is good and pure and fine and decent,
Where clouds are white and dolls and heaven
Surely is a white, white place with angels
Robed in white, and cotton candy and ice-cream
And milk and ruffled Sunday dresses
And dream houses and long sleek Cadillacs
And angel's food is white...all, all....white.

What can I say therefore, when my child
Comes home in tears because a playmate
Has called him black, big-lipped, flat-nosed
And nappy-headed? What will he think
When I dry his tears and whisper, "Yes, that's true.
But no less beautiful and dear"?
How shall I lift up his head, get him to square
His shoulders, look his adversaries in the eye,
Confident in the knowledge of his worth.

Serene under his sable skin and proud of his own beauty?
What can I do to give him strength,
That he may come through life's adversities
As a whole human being unwarped and human in a world of
Biased laws and inhuman practices that he might survive?
And survive he must! For who knows?
Perhaps this black child here bears the genius
To discover the cure for cancer
Or to chart the course for exploration of the universe...
So, he must survive for the good of all humanity.

He must and will survive.
I have drunk deeply of late from the fountain
Of my black culture, sat at the knee and learned
From Mother Africa, discovered the truth of my heritage.
The truth, so often obscured and omitted.
And I find I have much to say to my black children.

I will lift up their heads in proud blackness
With the story of their fathers and their father's fathers.
And I shall take them into a way back time
O Kings and Queens who ruled the Nile.
And measured the stars and discovered the
Laws of mathematics. Upon whose backs have been built
The wealth of two continents. I will tell him
This and more. And his heritage shall be his weapon
And his armor; will make him strong enough to win
Any battle he may face. And since this story is
Often obscured, I must sacrifice to find it
For my children, even as I sacrificed to feed,
Clothe and shelter them. So this will I do for them
If I love them. None will do it for me.
I must find the truth of heritage for myself
And pass it on to them. In years to come I believe
Because I have armed them with the truth, my children
And their children's children will venerate me.
For it is the truth that will make us free!

Man, Oh Man, How Wonderful You Are!

by
Angela J. Williams

In our wombs you were created
In God's image you were born
With just one look, we fell in love
And learned to love you more
A child, a teen, a young man,
Now, the man you've come to be
Through ups and downs, good times and bad
Yet you stand in victory
Tall, short, dark brown or light
No matter the size of frame
CEOs, doctors, plumbers, and more
And our love remains the same
We say with pride and honor you
For all you say and do
We're your mothers, wives, sisters,
Daughters, cousins, and girlfriends too
God's greatest work—this side of heaven
His best creation by far
You mighty, mighty, men of God
Man, Oh Man, How Wonderful You Are!

NOTES

Part I: The Prohecy

1. Ernest C. Sargent, III, *The Best Little Whore House in Jericho: Rahab and the Amazing Role of Blacks in Redemptive History*, International Apostolic Ministries, Forth Worth, TX, 2002, p. 29.

2. William D. McKissic, Sr., *Beyond Roots: In Search of Blacks in the Bible*, Renaissance Productions, Wenonah, NJ, 1990, p. 20.

3. McKissic, p. 16.

Part II: Christ-Centered Lessons From Biblical Black Characters

4. Anthony T. Evans and William D. McKissic, Sr., *Beyond Roots II: If Anybody Ask You Who I Am*, Renaissance Productions, Wenonah, NJ, 1990, p. 67.

5. Flavius Josephus, *Josephus: The Complete Works*, William A.M. Whiston (translator), Kregel Publications, Grand Rapids, MI, 1960, p. 31.

6. Arthur C. Custance, *Noah's Three Sons: Human History in Three Dimensions, Vol. 1*, The Doorway Papers, Zondervan Publishing House, Grand Rapids, MI, 1975, pp. 149–150.

7. Carlisle J. Peterson, *The Destiny of the Black Race,* Lifeline Communications, Toronto, Canada, 1991, pp. 336–337.

8. Kenneth A. Mathews, *The New American Commentary: Volume 1A Genesis 1–11:26*, Broadman & Holman Publishers, Nashville, TN, 1990 p.422.

9. Evans and McKissic, p. 92.

10. Derwin B. Stewart et al., *The African Cultural Heritage Topical: King James Version*, Pneuma Life Publishing, 1995, pp. 13–14.

11. McKissic, p. 23.

12. McKissic, p. 38.

13. McKissic, p. 49.

14. McKissic, pp.51–52.

15. John L. Johnson, *The Original Names and Descriptions of God and Jesus*, St. Louis, MO: Johnson Books, Inc., 2002, pp. 8–11.

16. In some late manuscripts, Acts 8:37: Philip said, "If you believe with all your heart, you may." The eunuch answered, "I believe that Jesus Christ is the Son of God."

17. Suzar Epps, *Blacked Out Through Whitewash, Volume I*, A-Kar Productions, Oak View, CA, 1999, p. 3.

18. Epps, p.3.

19. Epps, pp.57–58.

Part III: The Prayer of a Black Man Named Jabez (A Kenite)

20. Epps, pp.12, 13 and 14.

BIBLIOGRAPHY

Carlisle, John Peterson, *The Destiny of the Black Race*. Toronto, Canada: Lifeline Communications, 1991.

Custance, Arthur C. *Noah's Three Sons: Human History in Three Dimensions, Vol. 1, The Doorway Papers*. Grand Rapids, MI: Zondervan Publishing House, 1975.

Epps, Suzar. *Blacked Out Through Whitewash Volume I*, A-Kar Productions, Oak View, CA, 1999.

Evans, Anthony T. and William D. McKissic. *Beyond Roots II: If Anybody Asks You Who I Am*. Wenonah, NJ: Renaissance Productions, 1994.

Mathews, Kenneth A. *The New American Commentary: Volume 1A Genesis 1–11:26*, Nashville, TN: Broadman & Holman Publishers, 1990.

Johnson, John L. *The Black Biblical Heritage 14th Edition*. St. Louis, MO: Johnson Books, Inc., 2002.

------------. *The Original Names and Descriptions of God and Jesus*. St. Louis, MO: Johnson Books, Inc., 2002.

Josephus, Flavius. *Josephus: Complete Works*, William Whiston (translator). Grand Rapids, MI: Kregel Publications, 1960.

McKissic, William D. Sr. *Beyond Roots: In Search of Blacks in the Bible*. Wenonah, NJ: Renaissance, Productions, 1990.

Perryman, Wayne. *Thought Provoking Bible Studies of the 90s*. Washington, D.C.: Consultants Confidential Mercer Land, 1992, reprinted 1993.

Sargent, Ernest C. *The Best Little Whore House in Jericho: Rahab and the Amazing Role of Blacks in Redemptive History*. Fort Worth, TX: International Apostolic Ministries, 2002.

Stewart, Derwin B. et al. *The African Cultural Heritage Topical Bible: King James Version*. Bakersfield, CA: Pneuma Life Publishing, 1995.

Other Resources by George O. McCalep, Jr., Ph.D.
Committed to Doing Church God's Way

ORDER FORM

QTY	ITEM	EACH	TOTAL
	Faithful Over a Few Things	$ 19.95	$
	Faithful Over a Few Things—Study Guide	9.95	
	Faithful Over a Few Things—Audio Version	14.95	
	Faithful Over a Few Things—Resource Kit	189.95	
	Breaking the Huddle	14.95	
	Breaking the Huddle—Sermonic Audiocassette	10.00	
	Growing Up to the Head	19.95	
	Growing Up to the Head—Leader's Guide	10.95	
	Growing Up to the Head—Participant's Guide	10.95	
	Stir Up the Gifts	24.95	
	Stir Up the Gifts—Leader's Guide	10.95	
	Stir Up the Gifts—Workbook & Study Guide	10.95	
	Stir Up the Gifts—Sermonic Audio Series	19.95	
	Praising the Hell Out of Yourself	19.95	
	Praising the Hell Out of Yourself—Workbook	14.95	
	Praising the Hell Out of Yourself—CD	14.95	
	Praising the Hell Out of Yourself—T-Shirt (L, XL, XXL, XXXL)	10.00	
	Sin in the House	19.95	
	How to Be Blessed	19.95	
	"Jabez's Prayer"—Sermonic Audio Series	19.95	
	A Good Black Samaritan	3.95	
	Messages of Victory for God's Church in the New Millennium—Sermonic Audio Series	19.95	
	Tough Enough: Trials on Every Hand by Sadie T. McCalep, Ph.D.	20.00	
	Fulfillment Hour by Jackie S. Henderson & Joan W. Johnson, compiled and edited by George O. McCalep, Jr., Ph.D.	24.95	
	Faith Raising vs. Money Raising	24.95	
	When Black Men Stretch Their Hands to God	24.95	
	Subtotal		

Order by phone, fax, mail or online

Orman Press
4200 Sandy Lake Drive
Lithonia, GA 30038
Phone: 770-808-0999
Fax: 770-808-1955

www.ormanpress.com

ITEM	AMOUNT
Subtotal	
Postage & Handling (Call for Shipping Charges)	
C.O.D. (Add $6 plus Postage & Handling)	
Total	

Date_____Name_____

Address_____Apt./Unit_____

City_____State_____Zip_____

Credit Card #_____Exp. Date_____

Visit our web site @ www.ormanpress.com
Your one-stop store for Christian resources

Pastor and Sister McCalep are available to conduct workshops and seminars on all of these resources. Call 404-486-6740 for scheduling information.

THE AUTHOR'S COLLECTION

God has given me a burning passion for biblically based kingdom building and spiritual growth. Through His Spirit, I have discerned and recorded in my books discipleship principles related to church growth, evangelism, personal spiritual development, praise and worship. I recommend the following titles to those who are serious about *doing church God's way*.

Church Growth and Kingdom Building

Faithful Over a Few Things: Seven Critical Church Growth Principles bridges the gap between theory and practice. It offers seven principles that when faithfully implemented will cause your church to grow. The book is available in print and audio versions. A study guide and resource kit are also available. The resource kit contains a workbook, transparencies and a videotape.

Sin in the House: Ten Crucial Church Problems with Cleansing Solutions examines problems that hinder growth and offers proven solutions. This book addresses the question of why you and your church are not growing.

Fulfillment Hour: Fulfilling God's Purposes for the Church Through the Sunday School Hour by Jackie S. Henderson and Joan W. Johnson presents a nontraditional Sunday School model that fulfills all of the purposes and mission of the church through a systematic, balanced and creative approach within the context of an hour. *Fulfillment Hour* explains the concept, process and procedures of the model in detail. The model can be applied by any denomination and church.

Evangelism

Breaking the Huddle contains twelve messages that deal with the central theme of fulfilling Jesus' purpose of seeking and saving the lost (Luke 19:10). Like a football team, the church must break the huddle, that is, leave the comfort of the sanctuary and obediently go out among the unsaved to share the Gospel.

Stewardship

Faith Raising vs. Money Raising is the most complete stewardship resource available today. It presents a biblically-based approach to doing stewardship God's way. The book describes a proven stewardship plan that can be implemented in any church and any denomination. It also provides advice on how to raise capital for building projects and includes a study guide and teaching aid.

Personal Spiritual Development

Growing Up to the Head: Ten Essentials to Becoming a Better Christian challenges the reader to mature spiritually by growing up to the fullness of Christ. The study is based on the book of Ephesians. The book uniquely relates personal spiritual growth to numerical congregational growth. A new participant's guide and leader's guide are now available.

Stir Up the Gifts: Empowering Believers for Victorious Living and Ministry Tasks is a complete, practical guide on spiritual gifts that is applicable for any denomination. The book is based on 2 Timothy 1:6 where Paul tells us to stir up the gift and bring the fire to a flame. Study of this book will fire you up and revolutionize the ministries in your church. A leader's guide and study guide are available.

How to Be Blessed: Finding Favor with God and Man is a biblical guide to being blessed according to God's Word. It is based on the truth that God promises to bless His obedient children. This book will protect you from finding out too late about all the blessings that were yours, but you ever received.

Praise and Worship

Although the title is colorful, *Praising the Hell Out of Yourself* is a beneficial discipleship approach to praise and worship. It offers praise as an antidote for evil and provides the "how, why and when" of entering into His presence. A workbook, CD and T-shirt are available.

Inspiration

My wife's autobiography, *Tough Enough: Trials on Every Hand* describes how God transformed a shy, reserved, country girl from Alabama into a bold, self-assured, yet humble helpmeet to her husband and spokesperson for the Lord. Truly, you will be encouraged by her testimony of faith.

Black History

A Good Black Samaritan teaches biblical black history—specifically how Jesus used people of color to teach the world what is good.